BRIDGES FOR MODELLERS

A Brunel timber overbridge at Sonning Cutting on the Great Western Railway main line between London and Bristol.

British Rail

Bridge No. 1 on the London to Bedford line at St. Pancras, with new pointwork being laid on longitudinal timbers. This photograph shows a variety of different shaped main girders with a square trough type deck.

BRIDGES FOR MODELLERS

AN ILLUSTRATED RECORD OF RAILWAY BRIDGES

L.V. WOOD

Oxford Publishing Company

Typesetting by:
Aquarius Typesetting Services, New Milton, Hants.

Printed in Great Britain by:
Biddles Ltd., Guildford, Surrey.

Published by:
Oxford Publishing Co.
Link House
West Street
POOLE, Dorset

Acknowledgments

I would like to thank the Regional Civil Engineer, London Midland Region, for permission to prepare this volume, and also my friends throughout British Railways who have helped with information.

In addition, my thanks go to members of Milton Keynes Model Railway Society for their assistance and continued advice.

Contents

A variety of bridges on the approach to Acton Grange Viaduct over the Manchester Ship Canal. The first arch bridge (only partially visible) has stone voussoirs with brick spandrels; the second higher bridge has brick rings with masonry spandrels, etc., whilst the main span is now metallic. The original line was lower, to the right and, when the new deviation line caused by the construction of the Ship Canal was built, this led to an interesting combination.

British Rail

Foreword

Bridges have been featured by many famous photographers over the years. Examples which come to mind include the late Bishop Eric Treacy at Dent Station overbridge on the Settle & Carlisle line, and the late Maurice Earley with his photographs in Sonning Cutting and at the overbridge near Reading West. Other evocative photographs of trains passing under bridges have appeared over the years in the many published albums.

Unfortunately, whilst many good models of bridges exist, some, to a civil engineer, tend to make one wince, and it was with this in mind that I prepared this book. British Railways have over 65,000 bridges of 6ft. span or greater, and it is obviously very difficult to include a drawing or photograph of every type of bridge within this volume. However, I have attempted to show a reasonable cross section of average span bridges which could appear on model railway layouts. Few people have the space these days to produce multiple span viaducts and, in this case, most will visit a suitable structure to photograph and measure the structure.

Many photographs and drawings of British Railways' bridges are available from the BR/OPC Railprint scheme which is operated from OPC's Bournemouth shop. Sufficient information is given in this book for the modeller to be able to produce a reasonable model of a bridge, whilst personal observation can often spot details to produce a satisfactory model. I cannot emphasise too strongly that modellers should not trespass on British Rail's property thereby endangering their lives to obtain information, much of which is available at little cost.

Finally, I hope this book will act as an inspiration to modellers to have a go at constructing a bridge. There is certainly plenty to choose from!

L. Wood
1985

Introduction

In the case of the real railway, it should be remembered that the landscape existed before the railway arrived, and not as is usually the case with the modeller, first the baseboards, then the track, then the scenery. In other words, the whole programme of events back to front. So consider any railway which is to be constructed between two points, where no railway has existed before. Public rights of way, (roads, footpaths, bridle paths) as well as rivers, streams, canals and ditches, have to be crossed in the quest to provide a relatively level track bed across a landscape which is seldom flat, the track formation often being either on an embankment or in a cutting. Hence, the need for bridges and culverts to span any opening required.

In general railway practice, a bridge which carries the line over a river, road, etc., is termed an underline bridge (often abbreviated to underbridge) and, likewise, a bridge which carries a road over the railway is termed an overline bridge (overbridge). Where one railway line is carried over another line this is known as an intersection bridge.

Where existing narrow watercourses or ditches have been crossed by a new railway, these are termed culverts, which are often brick barrels, small brickarches or pipes. These generally are only up to about 6ft. (1.850 metres) wide. It is often very difficult to see these structures as they are frequently overgrown, and it is not unknown for them to provide a good home for wildlife, badger sets being particularly common. Often with changes in the use of the land, watercourses dry up, or in mining areas with subsidence, the watercourses will sometimes cause flows in alternative directions.

Most bridges tend to blend into the landscape well, and modellers should attempt to do the same. Most bridge designers attempt to produce pleasing designs to the eye, and it is perhaps worth mentioning here that all bridges, new or reconstructed, have their elevations approved by the appropriate local council prior to the necessary construction commencing on site.

Figure 1

8

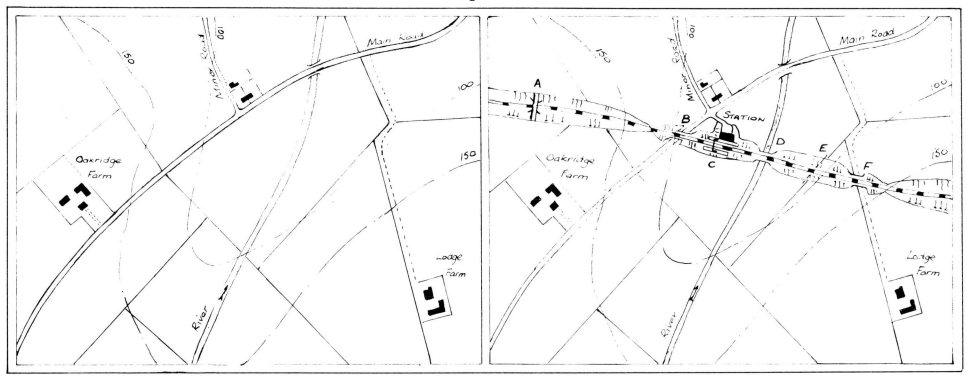

If we examine the map (**Figure 1**), the left-hand side shows a typical area of land, across which — on the right-hand side — a railway line has been built. The annotated right-hand map identifies the various types of bridges.

Bridge A
This bridge has been constructed because the farmer's land has been cut by the railway, and he would otherwise have no means of access to this field. This would be known as an accommodation bridge and the railway company would construct it for the farmer. It would be built to adequate capacity for his use. Should he sell the land on the other side, or require to take heavier loads across the structure, he would be required to pay for such works.

Bridge B
This would be a public bridge as the road existed prior to the railway being built.

Bridge C
The railway company, having built a new station, has provided a footbridge which would be classed 'private' by the railway.

Bridge D
This would be a new bridge to span the river. Were it known to be crossing the river's flood plain, it is possible that the railway company would construct a multiple span structure, even if normally the river only flowed through one span.

Bridge E
This structure would be a small culvert to carry water flowing along the ditch at the edge of the field.

Bridge F
This bridge would be constructed to carry the railway over the existing road to the farm. This is known as an occupation bridge, as the farmer would continue to have a right of way off his land to the main road.

Construction Depth

Depth is always the most important decision to be considered when the construction of a bridge is required. The construction depth dimension is illustrated in **Figure 2**.

In the case of underbridges, the headroom above a road or river (for navigation) is used, which together with the proposed construction depth of the structure, will enable the engineer to determine the required track level at that point. When all these details are available, a long section (track gradient profile) may be produced, showing the necessary earthworks involved.

Similarly for overbridges, the required railway headroom, including allowance for overhead electrification (if expected within the foreseeable future), will be provided, again giving road levels to the engineer. Coupled with the statutory requirements for vertical curves of roads, the approaches to the overbridge may then be established.

Bridge Spans

Three different bridge spans are often quoted on old Ordnance Survey sheets. If a bridge is built at other than 90 degrees to the track, it is termed a skew bridge and the angle of skew is measured as shown in **Figure 3**.

The spans, as illustrated, are self explanatory, but the other span sometimes quoted, and of more interest to the engineer, is that of the cross centres of the bearings. This is usually 4ft.-6ft. (1.850 metres) longer than the clear span, as this is the figure to which the bridge is designed. On a straight or non-skew bridge, obviously the clear and square spans are identical.

On masonry or brick arch bridges, no bearings exist and the span quoted is always that between abutments.

Without wishing to overburden the modeller with technicalities, it would perhaps be interesting to examine simply the effect of a load on a girder and arch type bridge, as this will help to illustrate why detail features of bridges exist.

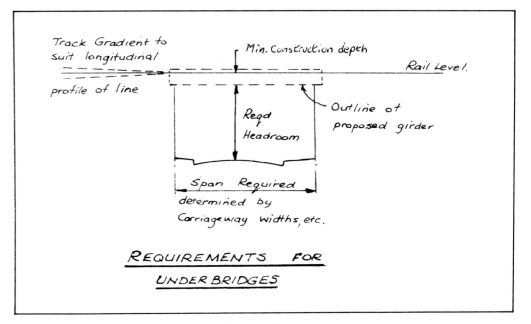

REQUIREMENTS FOR UNDERBRIDGES

Figure 2

Figure 3

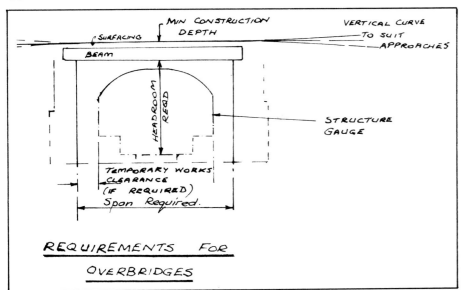

REQUIREMENTS FOR OVERBRIDGES

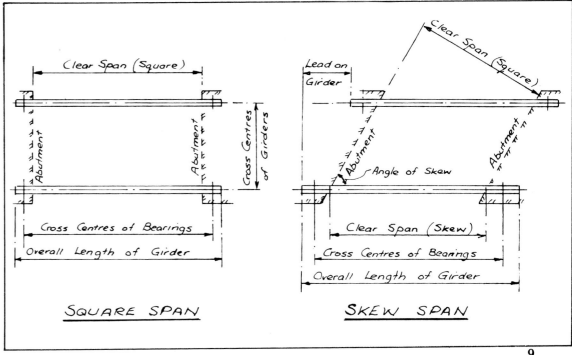

SQUARE SPAN

SKEW SPAN

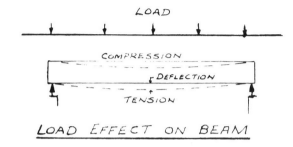

LOAD EFFECT ON BEAM

Figure 4a

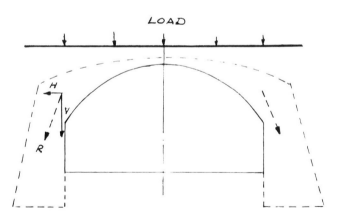

LOAD EFFECT ON ARCH

Figure 4b

In **Figure 4a**, the girders will tend to deflect, causing the top to be squeezed (compression) and the bottom to stretch (tension). In a girder, the flange plates take most of the force, due to the load moving across the bridge; the vertical web plate simply keeps the flange plates apart. As spans increase, additional flange plates, (called doubler flange plates) run for varying lengths of the girders as required.

As far as web plates are concerned, it is the reverse, particularly in riveted construction, where the web beomes thicker towards the ends of the girder, being joined behind the cover plate or stiffener.

The webs are only important at the ends to transfer the load (shear force) through the bearings to the abutments. All metallic girders are provided with stiffeners at the point of bearing to stiffen the web against buckling. These occur on both sides of the web for symmetrical girders.

A general guideline for plate girder bridges is that the depth of the web plate in inches should equal the cross centres of bearings in feet (e.g. for 36ft. cross centres of bearings, web depth would equal approximately 36in.). On metallic bridges, the temperature effect of expansion is taken up by having one end of a bridge's bearings fixed, and the other free. The fixed end of the bridge is firmly anchored, and it is here that the horizontal forces due to traction or the braking force of a train are absorbed to the abutment. At the free end, the bridge is free to move longitudinally but restrained laterally to resist the nosing forces (sideways motion) induced by trains (caused particularly by the reciprocating motion of steam engines).

In concrete beams, although not visible, additional reinforcement is placed at the bearings to absorb this vertical load.

In **Figure 4b**, illustrating the effect of a load on an arch bridge, very little deflection occurs, but the load beam forces are indicated. An arch is either sprung off rock or other stable ground, or has very substantial construction behind the abutment face. Needless to say, loss of this support to the arch will cause elongation, and as an arch relies on the compression (or strutting effect) between the abutments — since masonry or brickwork have relatively low tensile strength — loss of support will quickly lead to the collapse of the arch.

Clearances

All bridges, whether over or under the line, must be designed to clear the structure gauge as laid down by the legal requirements necessary to operate a railway. These basic clearances are shown in **Figure 5**.

It is also essential to provide parapets of suitable height to both under and over-footbridges, according to location.

Present requirements for underbridges are for a parapet height of 4ft. 6in. (1.370 metres) above walkway level (usually at the top flange level of the girder), of which the lower 12in. (0.305 metres) must be of solid construction.

On over-footbridges, the minimum parapet height is 4ft. 1in. (1.25 metres), but where any overhead electrical equipment is provided, this parapet height must be increased to 5ft. (1.500 metres). In this latter instance, the parapet must be of solid construction and have no hand or footholds. More recently, steeple copings (inverted 'V' units) have been applied to overbridges where lines have been electrified, to prevent easy access and to stop children (and adults!) endangering their lives.

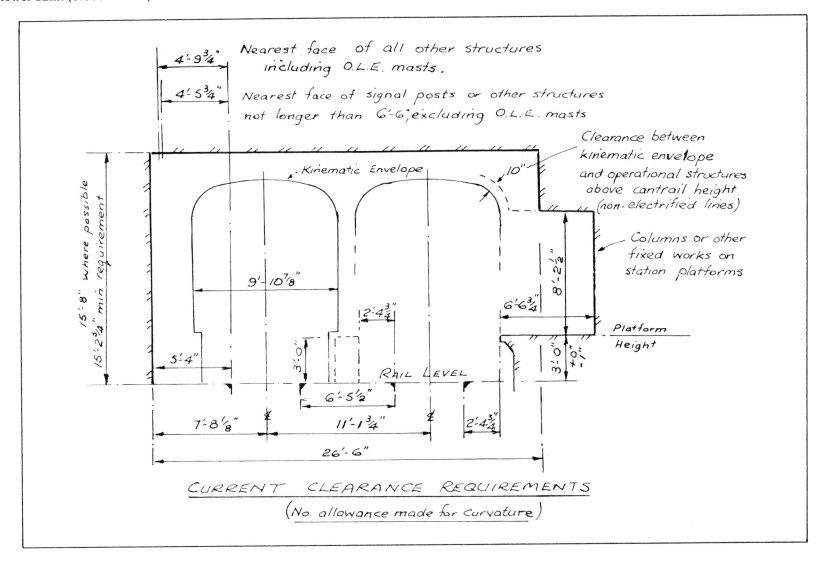

CURRENT CLEARANCE REQUIREMENTS

(No allowance made for curvature)

Figure 5

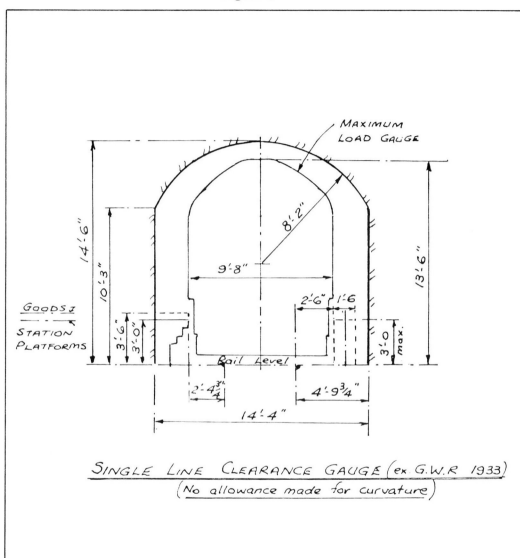

Figure 6

MAXIMUM LOAD GAUGE

14'-6"

10'-3"

8'-2"

9'-8"

13'-6"

GOODS STATION PLATFORMS

2'-6" 1'-6

3'-6"

3'-0"

Rail Level

3'-0 max.

2'-4¾"

4'-9¾"

14'-4"

SINGLE LINE CLEARANCE GAUGE (ex. G.W.R 1933)
(No allowance made for curvature)

(**Left**): A GWR overbridge near Chinnor, recently reconstructed. The bridge has only a 14ft. span.

L. Wood

(**Right**): A GWR ring elliptical overbridge at Aynho. This originally crossed the now removed headshunt.

L. Wood

Timber

Timber was extensively used in the construction of bridges for railways both for under and over-footbridges. Much of Brunel's early work was carried out using timber, with wrought-iron connectors and tie bars. If one of Brunel's timber viaducts in Devon or Cornwall is examined closely, it is obviously shaped as a series of arches with most of the load going straight down the masonry piers. However, substantial abutments would be provided to absorb the end thrust from the series of arches.

Landore Viaduct, near Swansea, was of similar construction until reconstructed in the 1890s with wrought-iron girders and a timber deck. Part of this timber viaduct was filled in with colliery waste to reduce the length, and following the hot summer of 1976, an underground fire burned for some considerable time beneath the track.

Timber viaducts also were used across estuaries, and the viaducts at Loughor (near Swansea) and Barmouth are well-known examples. Here, spans of about 15ft.-20ft. were utilised, with the rails carried on longitudinal timbers.

Timber has also been used for many years as a deck on all types of bridge. On underbridges, the timber usually spans between cross girders (i.e. is laid longitudinally) and would have a depth of 4in.-6in. (100-150 millimetres). Deeper timbers are used, particularly on deck span type bridges.

On overbridges, timber again is laid longitudinally on cross girders, and would then be covered with road metalling which would assist in spreading the load. Many footbridges have timber decks, usually spanning transversely between main girders seated on the bottom flange angle. The timbers are held down by a steel strap, which is coach-bolted through the timbers near the edges of the deck. Sometimes, these decks are covered with asphalt or a non-slip surface. Approach flights to many metallic footbridges are often constructed completely of timber.

Regrettably timber, however treated, absorbs water, and when placed adjacent to steel or wrought iron, inevitably leads to corrosion, however well the structure is maintained.

Concrete

Plain concrete (a mixture of sand/aggregate, cement and water) is seldom used in bridge work other than as a foundation below brick abutments, occasionally as a bedstone, or more frequently as a coping stone to tops of parapets or wing-walls. Concrete has a high compressive stress but has no resistance to any tensile force.

Reinforced Concrete

Reinforced concrete started to be used around 1900. Mild-steel bars are added on the tension side of the concrete, and any load causing tensile forces is assumed to be carried by the steel reinforcement, leaving the compressive forces to be taken care of by the concrete. In this way, spans up to about nine metres in length, particularly on overbridges, can be economically designed in reinforced concrete. The reinforcement is usually made up as a nest, wired together, and then placed in mould or shutters made of steel, timber or fibreglass, to produce the shape of the item required.

All reinforced sections rely on the distance of cover from the reinforcement to the outer surface of the concrete for its integrity, and any loss, or lack of cover, can lead to the reinforcement corroding and bursting out, causing spalling of the concrete surface.

Bedcourses or cill beams are often reinforced, but this is more often to prevent cracking during lifting on erection.

Pre-cast Post-Tensioned Reinforced Concrete

This type of beam was used in the early day of tensioning concrete. The beam is cast in the normal way, as for a reinforced beam, but then high tensile cables (or tendons), placed in sleeves and fixed in position to a known curve prior to casting, are tensioned after the concrete has reached a required compressive strength. By inducing this additional tension, it is possible to design more shallow beams than would be necessary if only wholly reinforced beams are used. At the same time, by raising the tendon at the bearings, a better spread of the vertical shear forces is possible. It is not essential to use a particularly high strength concrete in this system. After tensioning, the beam will normally assume a positive camber.

Pre-cast Pre-stressed Reinforced Concrete

When pre-stressed beams are produced, the high tensile wire strands (tendons) are tensioned on the casting bed, shutters are then placed around the tendons, and a high quality concrete is poured into the moulds. After curing, the tendons are cut at each end of the beam, and these are anchored (bonded) to the concrete, causing the concrete to compress. Again the beam assumes a positive camber.

Cast Iron

Cast iron, which had been used for weapons for many centuries, before first being used by Abraham Darby in the famous bridge at Coalbrookdale (opened in 1781), is produced by smelting iron ore in a furnace. Furnace limestone is added to the ore to remove or lift the impurities to the top, whilst the molten metal is run out of the bottom of the trough into moulds, formed generally in sand. The carbon content can vary from between 2 per cent and 6 per cent, which causes the cast iron to be brittle. Cast iron is normally relatively thick (never usually much less than one inch). This is necessary to enable the molten metal to flow into the mould, and remain molten until the mould is full, thereby cooling more slowly and reducing the possibility of cracking. Changes of section are gradual with substantial fillets in corners. Cast iron is very strong in compression, but is unable to withstand any tension (caused by bending). It is unusual for cast iron to corrode.

An early form of troughing formed in cast iron, known as the Barlow Rail, is shown in **Figure 7**, and was used for short span bridges on the GWR.

Wrought Iron

Wrought iron is produced from similar ore to that used for cast iron, but the carbon content is reduced to as low as 0.15 per cent, by smelting with substances containing oxygen. The molten metal is then cooled in lumps, and placed under a heavy hammer to consolidate the material and crush out other foreign matter. This lump (known as a bloom) is then reheated and rolled several times to produce a good quality iron. Rolled sections of joints, channels or angles may also be produced in this manner. The use of wrought iron in bridges stems from work carried out by Stephenson, Fairbairn, Hodgkinson and Clarke in the development of the rectangular tubes for the Conway and Britannia Bridges (built 1848 and 1850 respectively) in North Wales. The Britannia bridge has since been reconstructed, following a disastrous fire in 1970, with steel arches, and now carries a road above the railway. With the ability to roll much thinner material, this obviously reduced the dead weight of iron bridge structures. Wrought iron is an elastic material and, providing the material is not stressed beyond its elastic limit (about 24 tons per square inch), it should return to its original form after dynamic loading. Due to its manufacturing process, wrought iron tends to laminate when corrosion occurs. Construction is always by riveting, the holes being punched or drilled, but angle cranks to stiffeners are forged.

Mild Steel

Mild steel was a further development of wrought iron, the first bridge using mild steel being fabricated by the LNWR in 1879. Quality in the early days was inconsistent, and wrought iron was still used in bridges until about 1910. However, when Sir John Fowler and Sir Benjamin Baker designed the Forth Railway Bridge in 1890, steel was selected as the material. With the acceptance of steel for bridge construction, rolling mills were improved and became capable of rolling much larger plates than was previously possible. Thus it was possible for designers to lessen the number of cover plates to webs and flanges with the longer lengths available. By varying the chemical composition with the addition of manganese, nickel, additional carbon, etc., various qualities of steel are produced, which give good welding capability, unlike wrought iron which tends to laminate with the heat imput necessary to produce the weld. Mild steel tends to pit (small craters) when corroding, which will obviously tend to hole if the corrosion is left unchecked. Mild steel generally contains 0.2 per cent to 0.5 per cent carbon, and is produced in a similar manner to wrought iron, but has an improved elastic limit over wrought iron of about 30 per cent. All early steel bridges were of riveted construction, welded only becoming generally commonplace after 1948. It should be noted that only under exceptional circumstances is site welding ever undertaken. Welded construction allows the girders and floor units to be prefabricated, taken to site and bolted together. By using this technique, designers have been able to design bridges which can replace an existing structure in as little as a 24 hours possession of the line. Obviously such a technique requires a great deal of pre-planning, and this intense operation must of course take into account the largest unknown factor, the British climate.

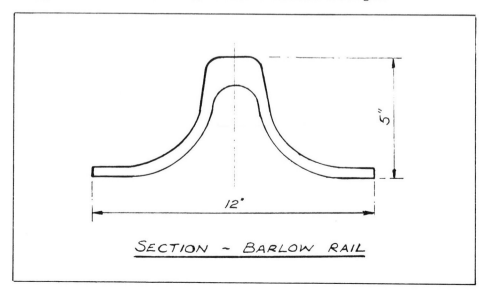

Figure 7

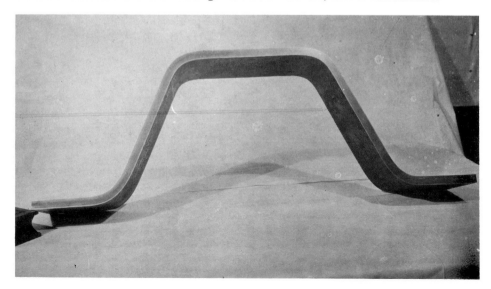

Figure 7a Section of Pressed Steel Troughing

Bridge Location and Reference

All regions of British Railways identify their various lines and branches by name, and bridges are numbered from the commencement of the line, except on the Western Region, where although the line is quoted, the nearest station (whether closed or not) and the mileage (including chainage) is quoted.

In those regions which use them, bridge numberplates are fixed on bridges, and several different varieties may be noted on the photographs of the various bridges in the book.

Bridge Number Plates (*Clockwise from right*): LMS cast-iron plate; BR flat plate with stencilled numerals; BR cast-iron plate; BR cast-iron plate on an ex-GWR bridge including the mileage from Paddington (86 miles 17 chains); LNWR cast-iron plate; LSWR cast-iron plate; BR cast-iron plate with suffix to aid identification where several bridges are adjacent.
L. Wood

15

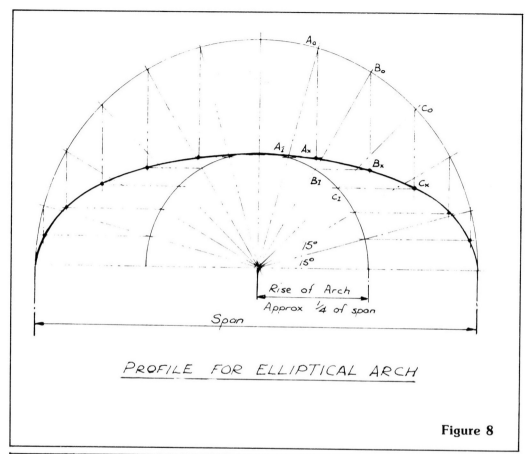

PROFILE FOR ELLIPTICAL ARCH

Figure 8

Arch Construction

Arches are formed to three different shapes, and the sketches in **Figure 8** indicate these. Also shown is the construction to produce an elliptical arch.

Figure 9

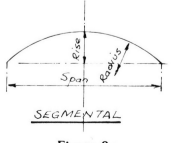

FORMS OF ARCH CONSTRUCTION

SEGMENTAL

Figure 9a

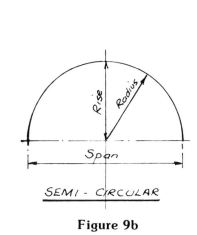

SEMI - CIRCULAR

Figure 9b

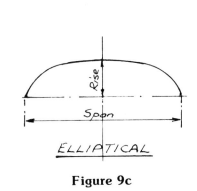

ELLIPTICAL

Figure 9c

17

Underbridges

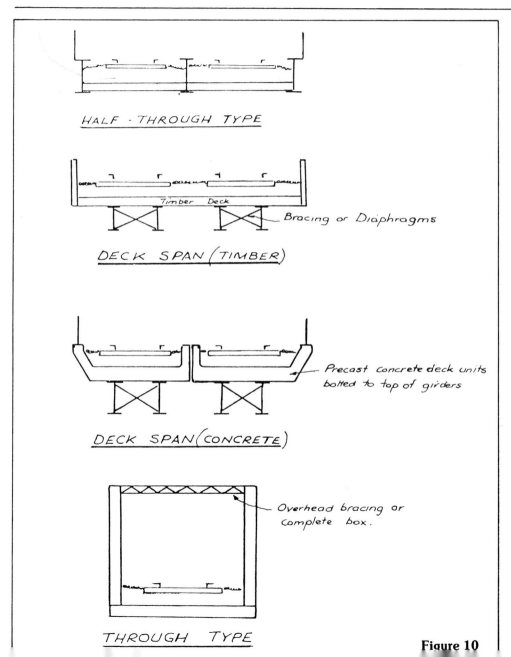

HALF-THROUGH TYPE

DECK SPAN (TIMBER)

Timber Deck

Bracing or Diaphragms

DECK SPAN (CONCRETE)

Precast concrete deck units bolted to top of girders

THROUGH TYPE

Overhead bracing or Complete box.

Figure 10

This section generally covers bridges carrying the railway, with spans exceeding 10ft. (3 metres). For spans of less than 10ft. see the section headed Culverts, Tunnels and Others.

It must be borne in mind that when most railway lines were constructed in this country, very little road traffic existed, and consequently most bridges were of relatively short spans (about 30ft. maximum) unless the railway actually had to cross a physical barrier such as a river or deep valley, where a major structure would often be required.

Many of the companies had standard designs for their bridges and these were used consistently over that railway area, variations only occurring where these designs proved unsuitable. To this day, British Rail have standard underbridge and overbridge designs which now appear in a variety of forms on all regions.

Early underbridges were constructed of masonry or brick arches of relatively small proportions, or cast-iron trough girders into which were placed the longitudinal timbers (these would only be suitable up to about 20ft. in span). With the increase of axle loads, cast iron, with its low tensile strength, started failing and a more suitable material, namely wrought iron, was produced, which could be rolled in plates. Many cast-iron arch underbridges still exist, particularly on the old Manchester South Junction & Altrincham route between Manchester and Altrincham. Generally, these exceed 60ft. in span, and some have been encased in reinforced concrete to strengthen the structures. Several bridges over the Grand Union Canal on the London to Rugby section of the ex-LNWR West Coast route have been treated in this manner, as has Radcliffe Viaduct over the River Trent between Nottingham and Grantham. Another graceful double-arch bridge exists on the ex-GWR Didcot to Chester line, south of Shrewsbury, where the River Severn is crossed by the Belvidere Bridge. Several cast-iron viaducts were constructed, and most, like Crumlin (GWR) and Belah (NER), have been demolished.

CLASSIFICATION OF UNDERBRIDGES

This shows a small three ring arch which would be satisfactory for spans up to about 20ft.

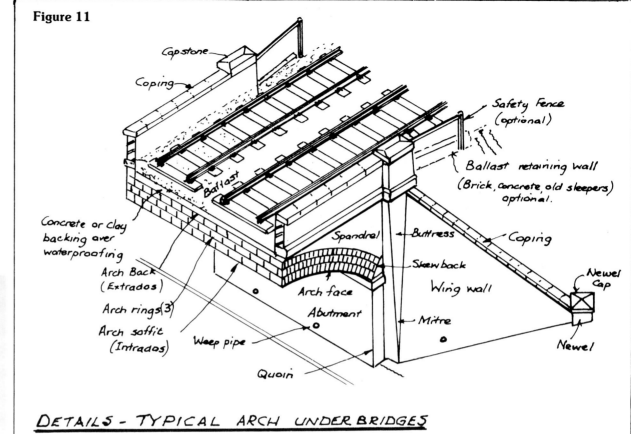

Figure 11

Capstone

Coping

Safety Fence (optional)

Ballast retaining wall (Brick, concrete, old sleepers) optional.

Ballast

Concrete or clay backing over waterproofing

Spandrel

Buttress

Coping

Arch Back (Extrados)

Skewback

Arch face

Wing wall

Newel Cap

Arch rings (3)

Abutment

Mitre

Arch soffit (Intrados)

Weep pipe

Newel

Quoin

DETAILS - TYPICAL ARCH UNDER BRIDGES

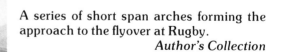

A series of short span arches forming the approach to the flyover at Rugby.

Author's Collection

19

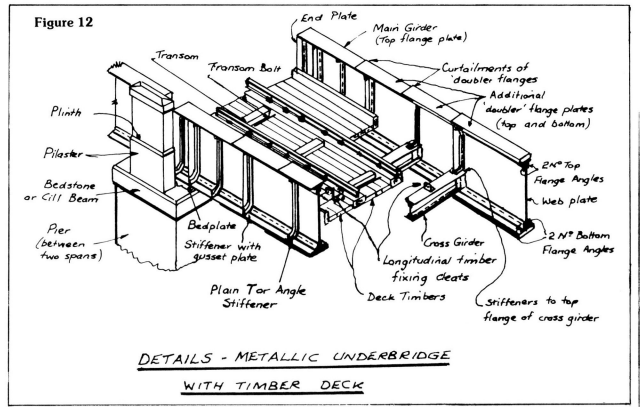

Figure 12

End Plate

Main Girder
(Top flange plate)

Transom

Transom Bolt

Curtailments of
'doubler' flanges

Additional
'doubler' flange plates
(top and bottom)

Plinth

Pilaster

Bedstone
or Cill Beam

2 N° Top
Flange Angles

Web plate

Pier
(between
two spans)

Bedplate

Stiffener with
gusset plate

Cross Girder

2 N° Bottom
Flange Angles

Longitudinal timber
fixing cleats

Plain Tor Angle
Stiffener

Deck Timbers

stiffeners to top
flange of cross girder

DETAILS - METALLIC UNDERBRIDGE

WITH TIMBER DECK

A metallic bridge, main girders with cross girders, longitudinal timbers with timber deck.

Another view of Bridge No. 1 at St. Pancras, showing the longitudinal timber trackbed and timber walkways.

British Rail

A further metallic bridge, this time with main girders, cross girders and railbearers. This could have a timber deck with longitudinal timbers fixed to the railbearer, although in this case a steel plate deck is used. Cross girders would normally occur at 4ft.-6ft. cross centres, although on some bridges much larger centres with deeper railbearers can exist.

Figure 13

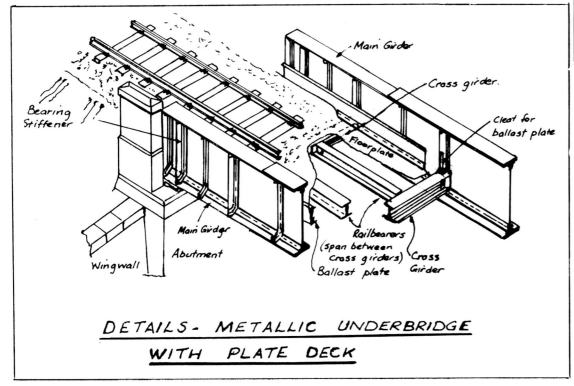

DETAILS - METALLIC UNDERBRIDGE
WITH PLATE DECK

Metallic span with cantilevered parapet, forming part of the viaduct approach to Nottingham Victoria (built 1898).

Lattice girder type deck span with two semicircular approach spans (near Warrington).

Figure 14

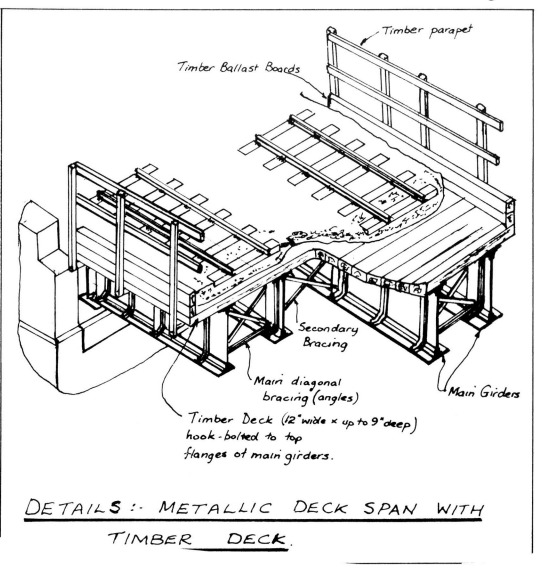

Timber parapet

Timber Ballast Boards

Secondary Bracing

Main diagonal bracing (angles)

Timber Deck (12"wide × up to 9"deep) hook-bolted to top flanges of main girders.

Main Girders

A typical metallic deck span (the deck is supported off the tops of the main girders). The main girders are braced together to support each track, and sometimes secondary bracing occurs between the inner girders. A timber deck is shown in this case, but pre-cast concrete units can also be used.

DETAILS:- METALLIC DECK SPAN WITH TIMBER DECK.

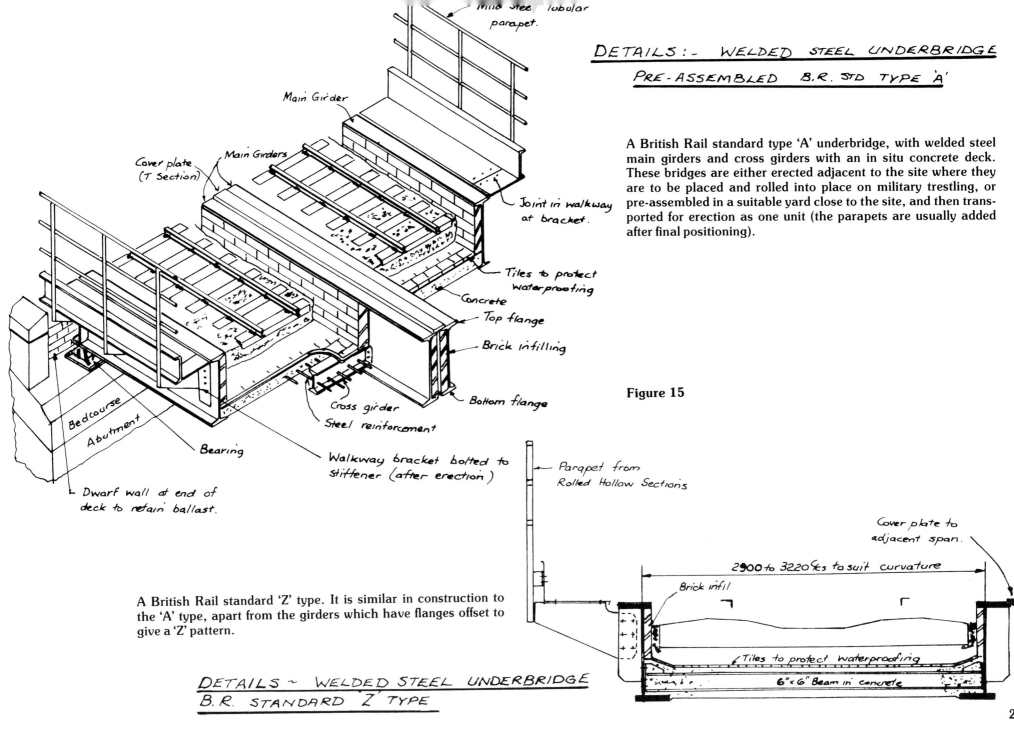

Mild steel tubular parapet.

Main Girder

Main Girders

Cover plate (T Section)

Joint in walkway at bracket.

Tiles to protect waterproofing

Concrete

Top flange

Brick infilling

Bottom flange

Cross girder

Steel reinforcement

Bedcourse

Abutment

Bearing

Walkway bracket bolted to stiffener (after erection)

Dwarf wall at end of deck to retain ballast.

DETAILS:- WELDED STEEL UNDERBRIDGE

PRE-ASSEMBLED B.R. STD TYPE 'A'

A British Rail standard type 'A' underbridge, with welded steel main girders and cross girders with an in situ concrete deck. These bridges are either erected adjacent to the site where they are to be placed and rolled into place on military trestling, or pre-assembled in a suitable yard close to the site, and then transported for erection as one unit (the parapets are usually added after final positioning).

Figure 15

Parapet from Rolled Hollow Sections

Cover plate to adjacent span.

2900 to 3220 Ctrs to suit curvature

Brick infil

Tiles to protect waterproofing

6"x 6" Beam in concrete

A British Rail standard 'Z' type. It is similar in construction to the 'A' type, apart from the girders which have flanges offset to give a 'Z' pattern.

DETAILS ~ WELDED STEEL UNDERBRIDGE

B.R. STANDARD 'Z' TYPE

23

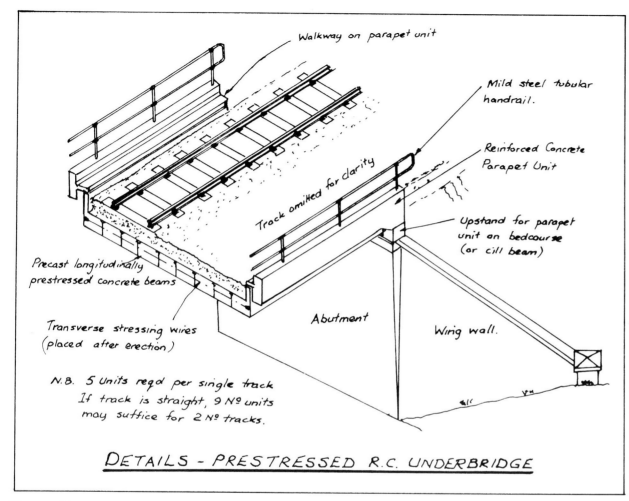

Walkway on parapet unit

Mild steel tubular handrail.

Reinforced Concrete Parapet Unit

Track omitted for clarity

Upstand for parapet unit on bedcourse (or cill beam)

Precast longitudinally prestressed concrete beams

Abutment

Wing wall.

Transverse stressing wires (placed after erection)

N.B. 5 Units req'd per single track
If track is straight, 9 N° units may suffice for 2 N° tracks.

DETAILS - PRESTRESSED R.C. UNDERBRIDGE

Figure 16

A standard British Rail pattern rectangular pre-stressed concrete bridge, satisfactory where adequate construction depth is available. Because of the additional weight it requires substantial abutments. (see Figure 47).

An example of this type of bridge near Saunderton. The pockets along the lower beams are the points of transverse stressing wires, which hold the deck together to act as a complete slab.

L. Wood

Figure 17

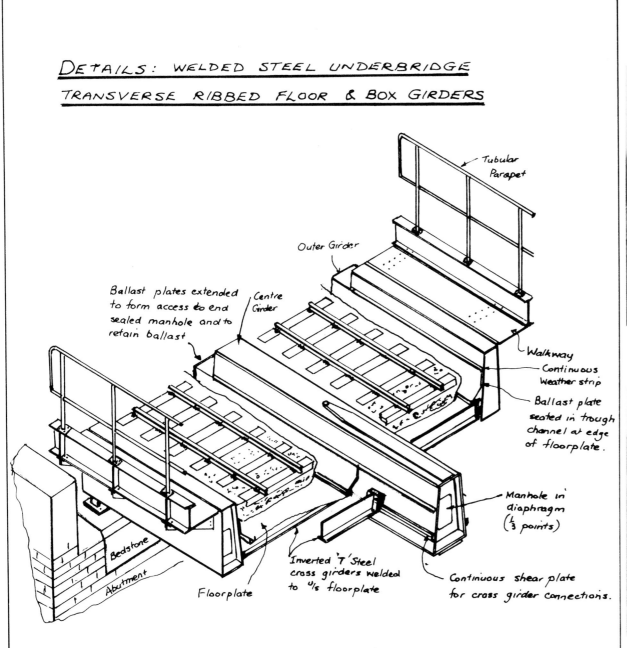

DETAILS: WELDED STEEL UNDERBRIDGE

TRANSVERSE RIBBED FLOOR & BOX GIRDERS

Tubular Parapet

Outer Girder

Ballast plates extended to form access to end sealed manhole and to retain ballast

Centre Girder

Walkway

Continuous Weather strip

Ballast plate seated in trough channel at edge of floorplate.

Manhole in diaphragm ($\frac{1}{3}$ points)

Bedstone

Abutment

Floorplate

Inverted 'T' Steel cross girders welded to u/s floorplate

Continuous shear plate for cross girder connections.

Developed by the Western Region, this form of box girder underbridge is now also appearing on other regions. Welded steel girders and floor units (which can be up to 40ft. long) can be erected quickly in short time periods by reducing the numbers of lifts involved (**see also Figures 49 to 51**).

A single line box girder bridge, constructed in 1970, over a realigned road near Bledlow.

L. Wood

Figure 17a Metallic girders with cross girders and a plate deck with longitudinal timbers.

Figure 17b Trial erection in the workshops of Fairfield Shipbuilding & Eng. Co. at Chepstow. The bridge is a late 1950s style Western Region underbridge consisting of welded plate girders, welded floor units and an intermediate trough unit for drainage.

Figure 17c A short span semicircular arch bridge, near Penrith, on the Lancaster & Carlisle main line.

Figure 17d A GWR through type lattice bridge with overhead bracing.

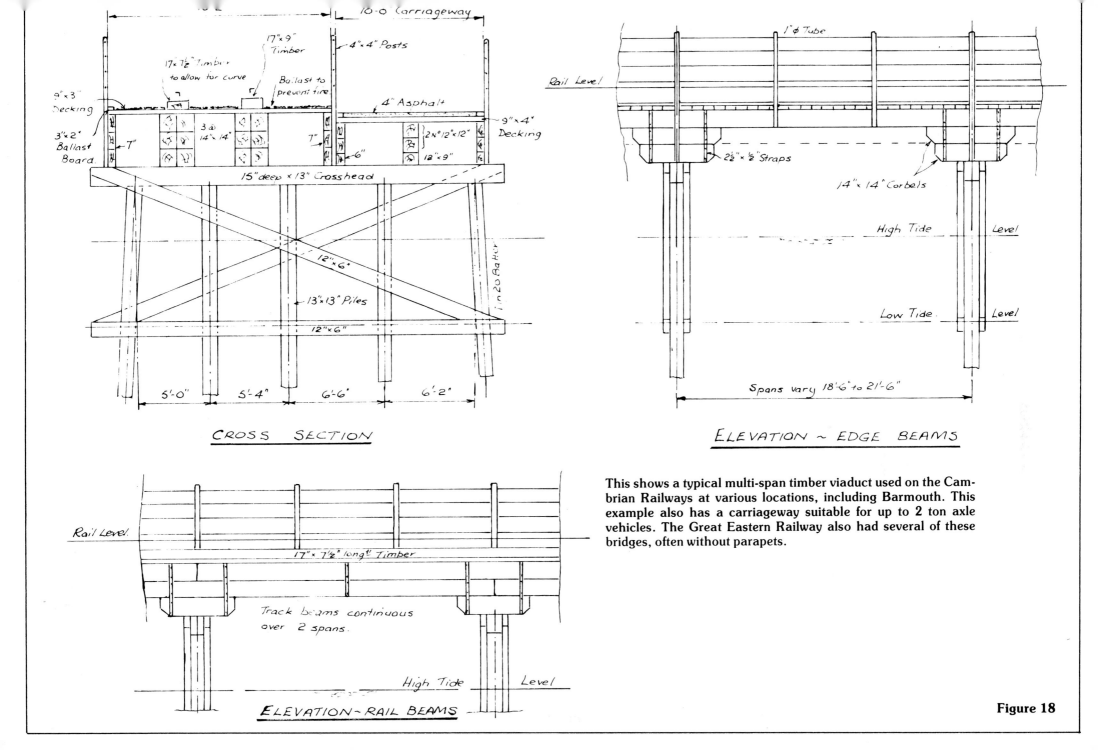

CROSS SECTION

10-0 Carriageway

17"x 7½" Timber to allow for curve

17"x 9" Timber

4"x 4" Posts

Ballast to prevent fire

4" Asphalt

9"x 3" Decking

3"x 2" Ballast Board

9"x 4" Decking

3 @ 14"x 14"

2 N° 12"x 12"

12"x 9"

7"

6"

7"

15" deep x 13" Crosshead

12"x 6"

13"x 13" Piles

12"x 6"

1 in 20 Batter

5'-0"   5'-4"   6'-6"   6'-2"

ELEVATION ~ EDGE BEAMS

Rail Level

1"ø Tube

2½"x ½" Straps

14"x 14" Corbels

High Tide Level

Low Tide Level

Spans vary 18'-6" to 21'-6"

ELEVATION ~ RAIL BEAMS

Rail Level

17"x 7½" long¹ Timber

Track beams continuous over 2 spans.

High Tide Level

This shows a typical multi-span timber viaduct used on the Cambrian Railways at various locations, including Barmouth. This example also has a carriageway suitable for up to 2 ton axle vehicles. The Great Eastern Railway also had several of these bridges, often without parapets.

Figure 18

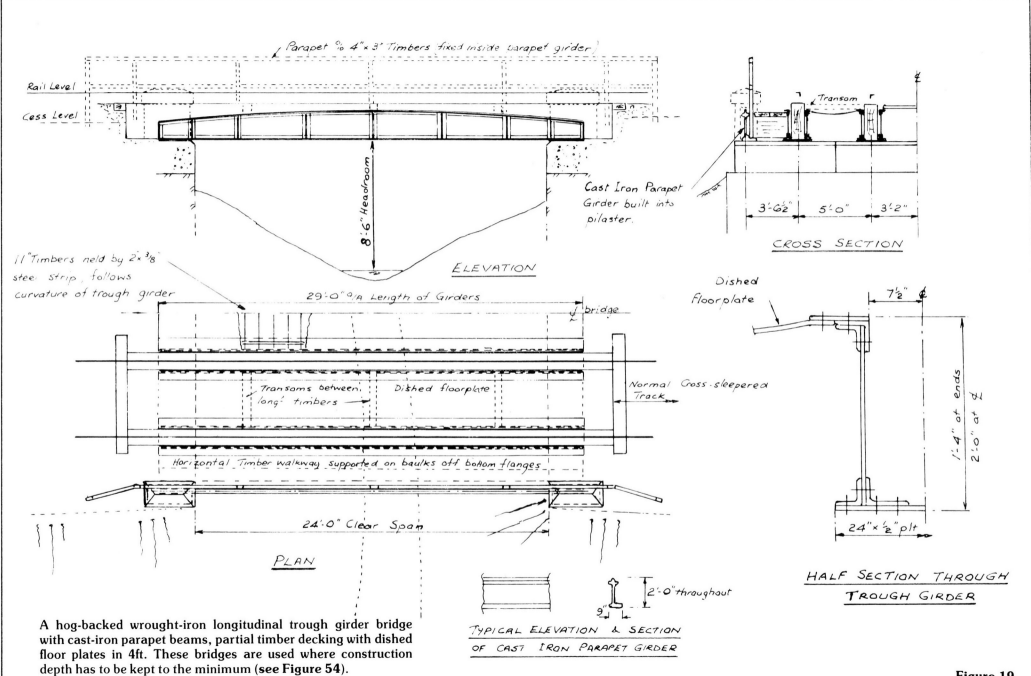

Parapet % 4"x 3" Timbers fixed inside parapet girder)

Rail Level

Cess Level

8'-6" Headroom

ELEVATION

Cast Iron Parapet Girder built into pilaster.

Transom

CROSS SECTION

3'-6½"   5'-0"   3'-2"

II" Timbers held by 2"× ³/₈ steel strip, follows curvature of trough girder

29'-0" %a Length of Girders

¢ bridge

Transoms between long¹ timbers

Dished floorplate

Normal Cross-sleepered Track

Horizontal Timber walkway supported on baulks off bottom flanges

24'-0" Clear Span

PLAN

Dished Floorplate

7½"   ¢

1'-4" at ends

2'-0" at ¢

24"× ½" plt

HALF SECTION THROUGH TROUGH GIRDER

2'-0" throughout

9"

TYPICAL ELEVATION & SECTION OF CAST IRON PARAPET GIRDER

A hog-backed wrought-iron longitudinal trough girder bridge with cast-iron parapet beams, partial timber decking with dished floor plates in 4ft. These bridges are used where construction depth has to be kept to the minimum (**see Figure 54**).

Figure 19

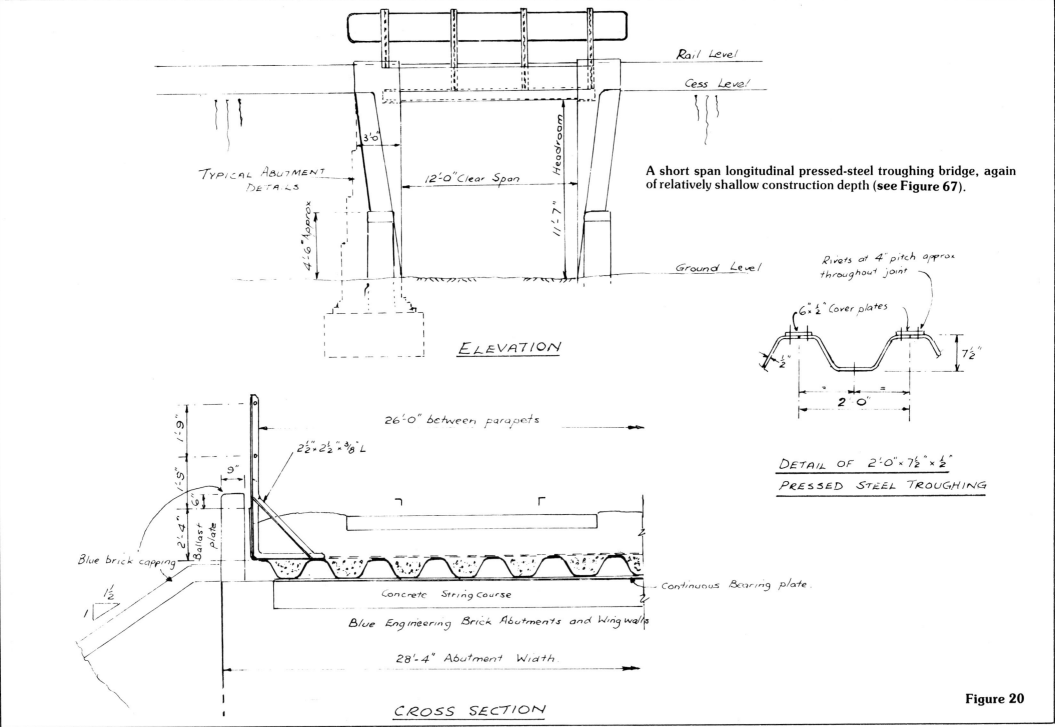

Rail Level

Cess Level

TYPICAL ABUTMENT
DETAILS

3'0"

12'-0" Clear Span

Headroom

11'-7"

4'-6" Approx

Ground Level

A short span longitudinal pressed-steel troughing bridge, again of relatively shallow construction depth (see Figure 67).

ELEVATION

Rivets at 4" pitch approx throughout joint

6" x ½" Cover plates

7½"

2'0"

DETAIL OF 2'-0" x 7½" x ½"
PRESSED STEEL TROUGHING

26'-0" between parapets

1'-9"

1'-5"

9"

2½" x 2½" x ⅜" L

6"

2'-4"

Ballast plate

Blue brick capping

1½"

1

Concrete String Course

Continuous Bearing plate.

Blue Engineering Brick Abutments and Wing walls

28'-4" Abutment Width.

CROSS SECTION

Figure 20

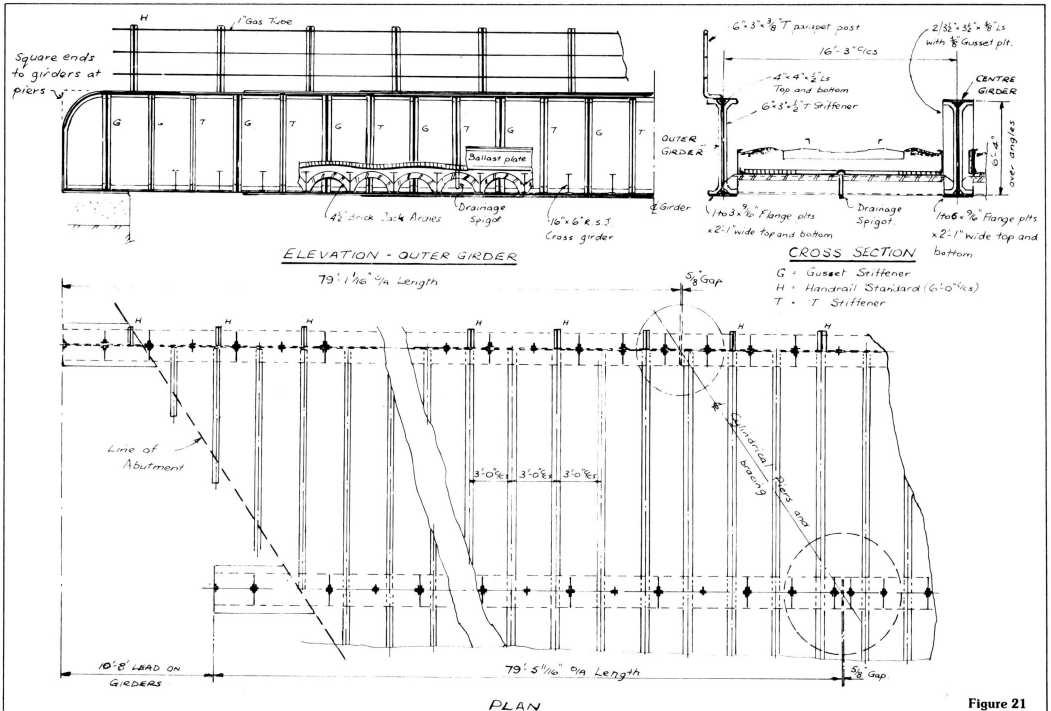

ELEVATION - OUTER GIRDER

79'-1 1/16" o/a Length

CROSS SECTION

G = Gusset Stiffener
H = Handrail Standard (6'-0"c/cs)
T = T Stiffener

PLAN

Figure 21

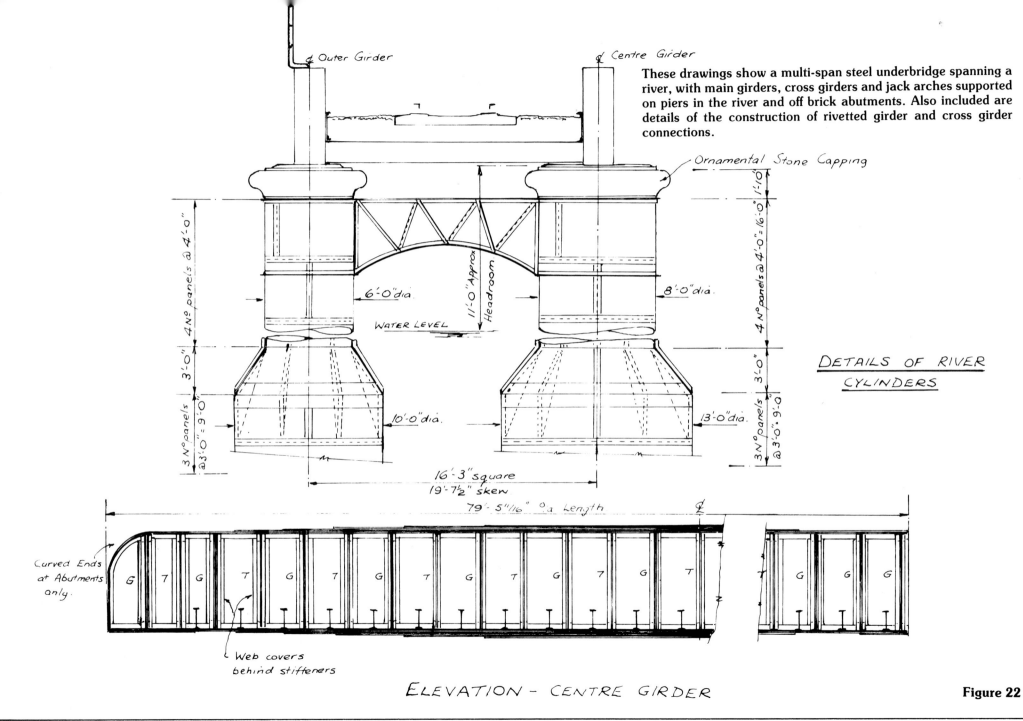

d Outer Girder

d Centre Girder

These drawings show a multi-span steel underbridge spanning a river, with main girders, cross girders and jack arches supported on piers in the river and off brick abutments. Also included are details of the construction of rivetted girder and cross girder connections.

Ornamental Stone Capping

4 N° panels @ 4'-0"
3'-0"
3 N° panels @ 3'-0" = 9'-0"

4 N° panels @ 4'-0" = 16'-0" 1'-0"
3'-0"
3 N° panels @ 3'-0" = 9'-0"

6'-0"dia

8'-0"dia.

11'-0" Approx Headroom

WATER LEVEL

10'-0"dia.

13'-0"dia.

DETAILS OF RIVER CYLINDERS

16'-3" square
19'-7½" skew

79'-5"¹¹⁄₁₆" Oa Length

Curved Ends at Abutments only.

G 7 G 7 G 7 G 7 G 7 G 7 G 7 G G G

Web covers behind stiffeners

ELEVATION - CENTRE GIRDER

Figure 22

31

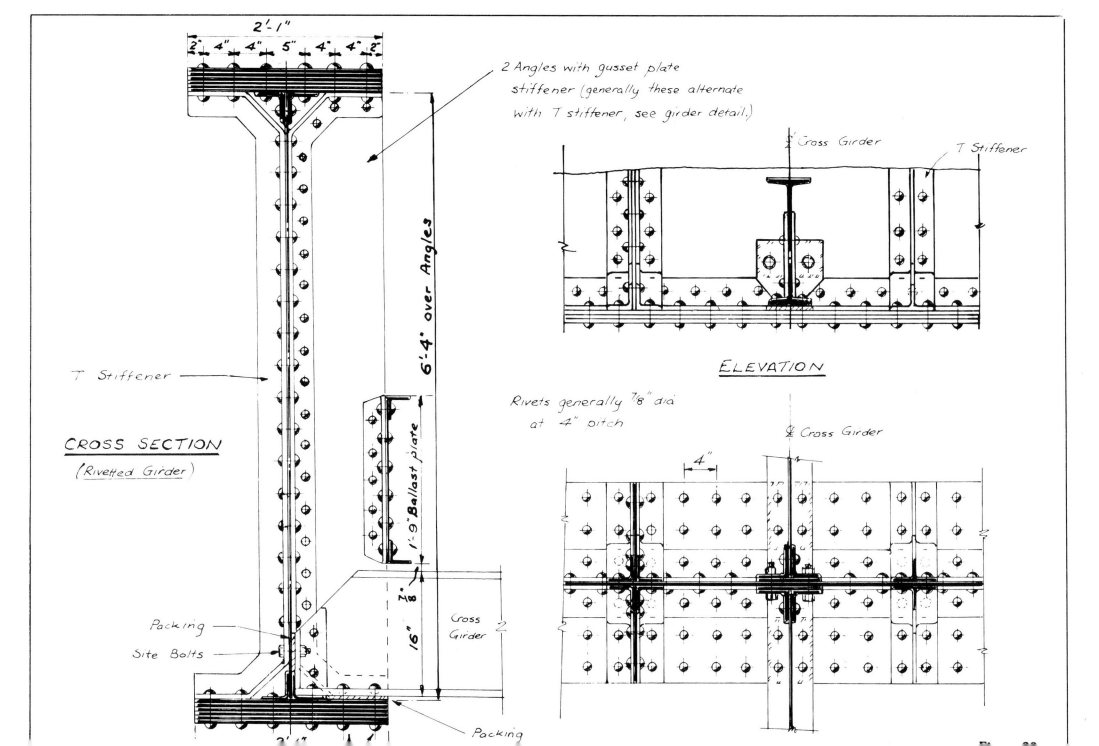

2'-1"

2" 4" 4" 5" 4" 4" 2"

2 Angles with gusset plate
stiffener (generally these alternate
with T stiffener, see girder detail.)

6'-4" over Angles

T Stiffener

1'-9" Ballast plate

CROSS SECTION

(Rivetted Girder)

Packing

Site Bolts

7"
8

16"

Cross
Girder 2

3'-1"

Packing

℄ Cross Girder

T Stiffener

ELEVATION

Rivets generally 7/8" dia
at 4" pitch

4"

℄ Cross Girder

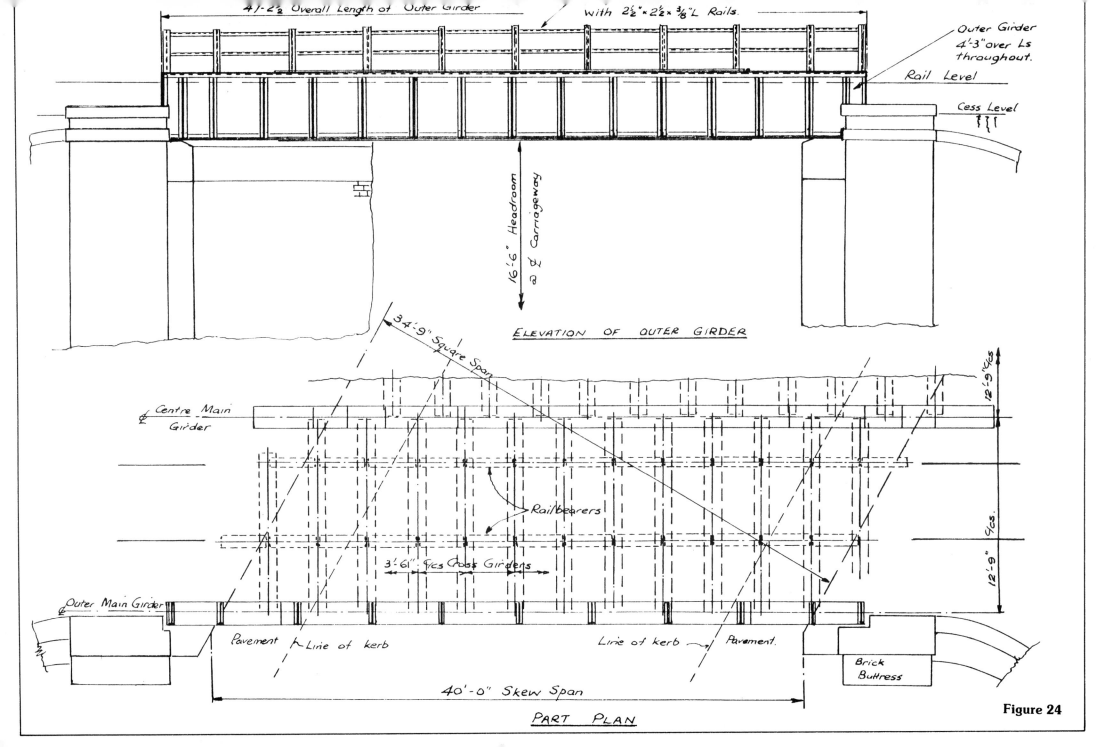

41'-2½" Overall Length of Outer Girder

With 2½" × 2½" × ⅜" L Rails.

Outer Girder
4'-3" over Ls
throughout.

Rail Level

Cess Level

16'-6" Headroom @ ℄ Carriageway

ELEVATION OF OUTER GIRDER

34'-9" Square Span

12'-9" ℄cs

℄ Centre Main Girder

Railbearers

12'-9" ℄cs.

3'-6½" ℄cs Cross Girders

Outer Main Girder

Pavement   Line of kerb   Line of kerb   Pavement.

Brick Buttress

40'-0" Skew Span

PART PLAN

Figure 24

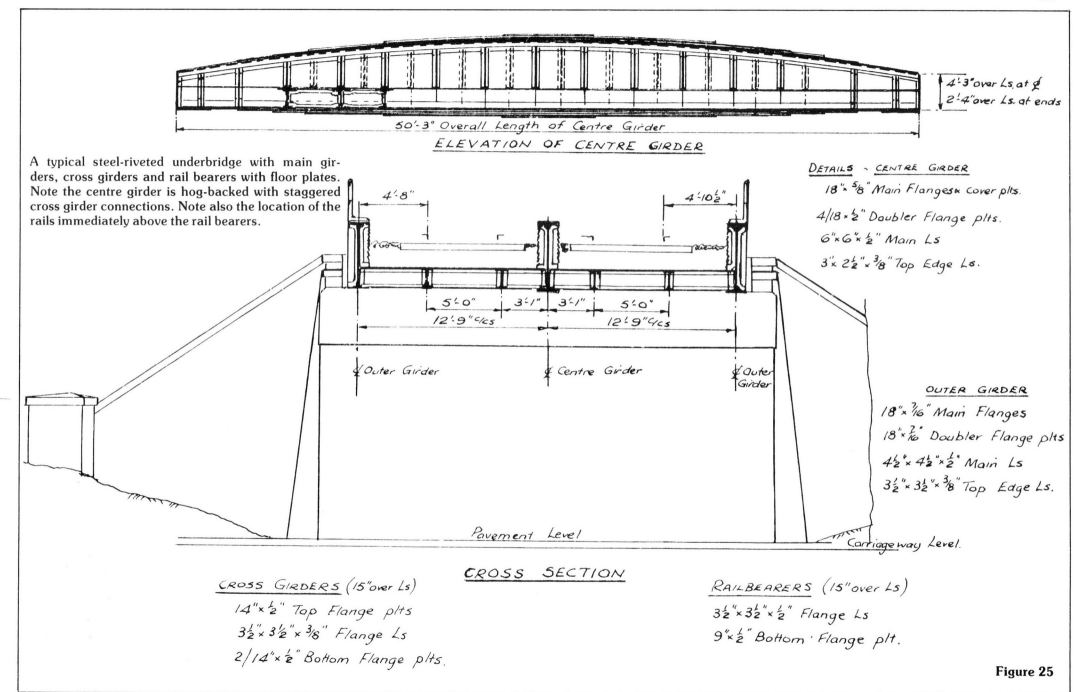

4'-3" over Ls. at ℄
2'-4" over Ls. at ends

50'-3" Overall Length of Centre Girder

ELEVATION OF CENTRE GIRDER

A typical steel-riveted underbridge with main girders, cross girders and rail bearers with floor plates. Note the centre girder is hog-backed with staggered cross girder connections. Note also the location of the rails immediately above the rail bearers.

4'-8"

4'-10½"

DETAILS ~ CENTRE GIRDER

18" × ⅝" Main Flanges & cover plts.

4/18 × ½" Doubler Flange plts.

6" × 6" × ½" Main Ls

3" × 2½" × ⅜" Top Edge Ls.

5'-0"   3'-1"   3'-1"   5'-0"

12'-9" c/cs   12'-9" c/cs

℄ Outer Girder   ℄ Centre Girder   ℄ Outer Girder

OUTER GIRDER

18" × ⁷⁄₁₆" Main Flanges

18" × ²⁄₁₆" Doubler Flange plts

4½" × 4½" × ½" Main Ls

3½" × 3½" × ⅜" Top Edge Ls.

Pavement Level

Carriageway Level.

CROSS SECTION

CROSS GIRDERS (15" over Ls)

14" × ½" Top Flange plts

3½" × 3½" × ⅜" Flange Ls

2/14" × ½" Bottom Flange plts.

RAILBEARERS (15" over Ls)

3½" × 3½" × ½" Flange Ls

9" × ½" Bottom Flange plt.

Figure 25

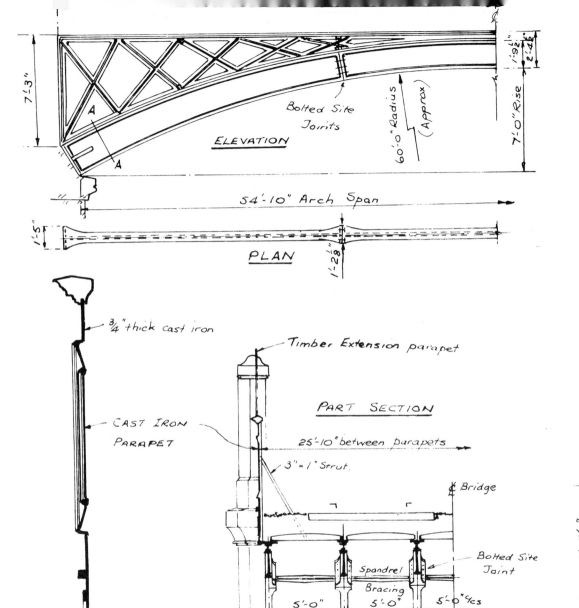

ELEVATION

7'-3"

Bolted Site Joints

60'-0" Radius (Approx)

7'-0" Rise

1'-9½" 2'-4½"

54'-10" Arch Span

1'-5"

PLAN

1-28½"

¾" thick cast iron

CAST IRON PARAPET

Fixing to edge beam

Timber Extension parapet

PART SECTION

25'-10" between parapets

3"×1" Strut

℄ Bridge

Bolted Site Joint

Spandrel Bracing

5'-0" 5'-0" 5'-0" %cs

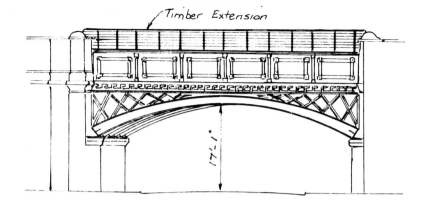

Timber Extension

ELEVATION

17'-1"

N.B. Spandrel members and bracing are of cruciform section ✚.

Details of a cast-iron arch with spandrel bracing. Note again the arch ribs. In early days, longitudinal timbers were located in the gap between the cast floor plates prior to the cross-sleepered ballasted track being laid (see Figures 44, 45 & 47).

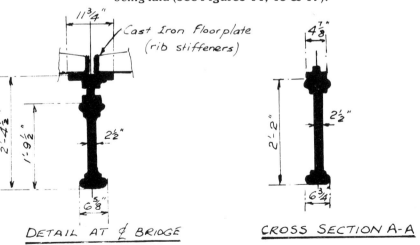

Cast Iron Floorplate (rib stiffeners)

11¾"

2'-4½" 1'-9½" 2½"

5⅝"

DETAIL AT ℄ BRIDGE

4⅞"

2'-2" 2½"

6¾"

CROSS SECTION A-A

Figure 26

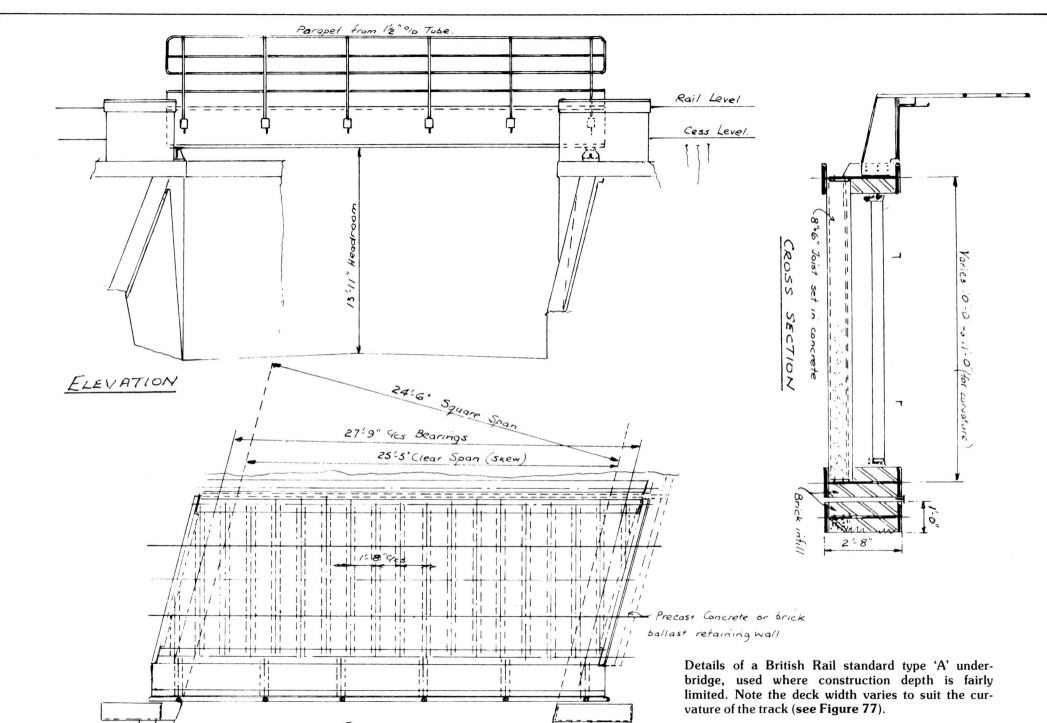

Parapet from 1½" ⌀ Tube.

Rail Level

Cess Level.

13'-11" Headroom

ELEVATION

24'-6" Square Span

27'-9" C/cs Bearings

25'-5" Clear Span (skew)

1'-8" C/cs

Precast Concrete or brick ballast retaining wall

CROSS SECTION

8"×6" Joist set in concrete

Varies :0'-0" 3.11-0" (for curvature)

Brick infill

1'-0"

2'-8"

Details of a British Rail standard type 'A' under-bridge, used where construction depth is fairly limited. Note the deck width varies to suit the curvature of the track (see **Figure 77**).

Figure 97

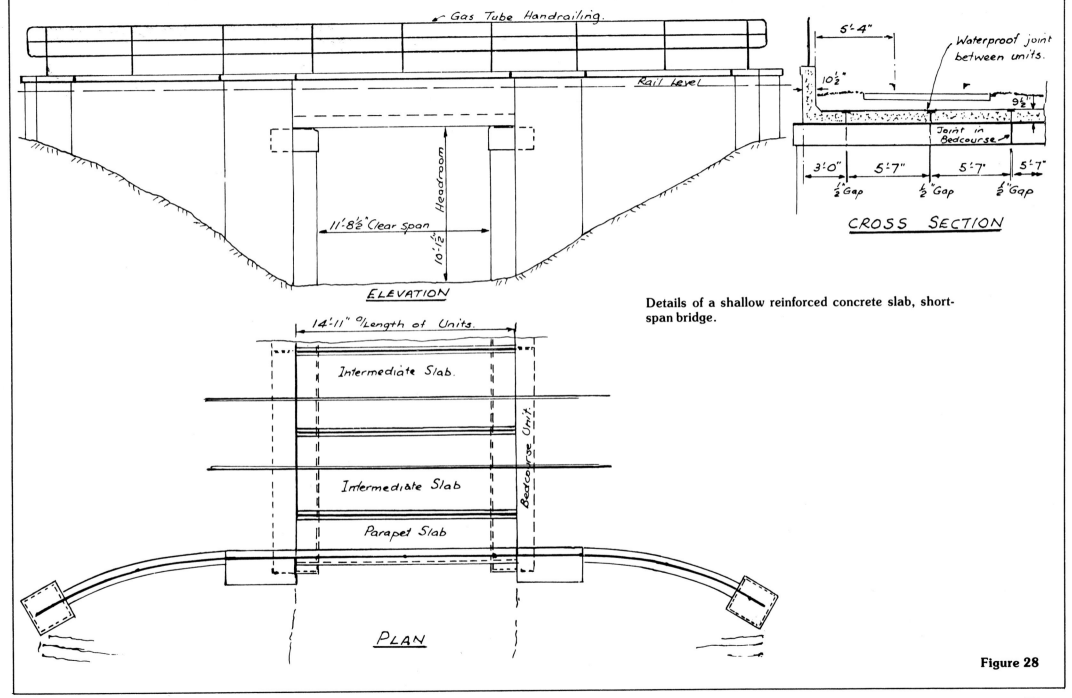

Gas Tube Handrailing.

Rail Level

11'-8½" Clear Span

10'-1½" Headroom

ELEVATION

5'-4"

10½"

Waterproof joint between units.

9½"

Joint in Bedcourse

3'-0"   5'-7"   5'-7"   5'-7"
½" Gap   ½" Gap   ½" Gap

CROSS SECTION

Details of a shallow reinforced concrete slab, short-span bridge.

14'-11" O/Length of Units.

Intermediate Slab.

Intermediate Slab

Parapet Slab

Bedcourse Unit.

PLAN

Figure 28

37

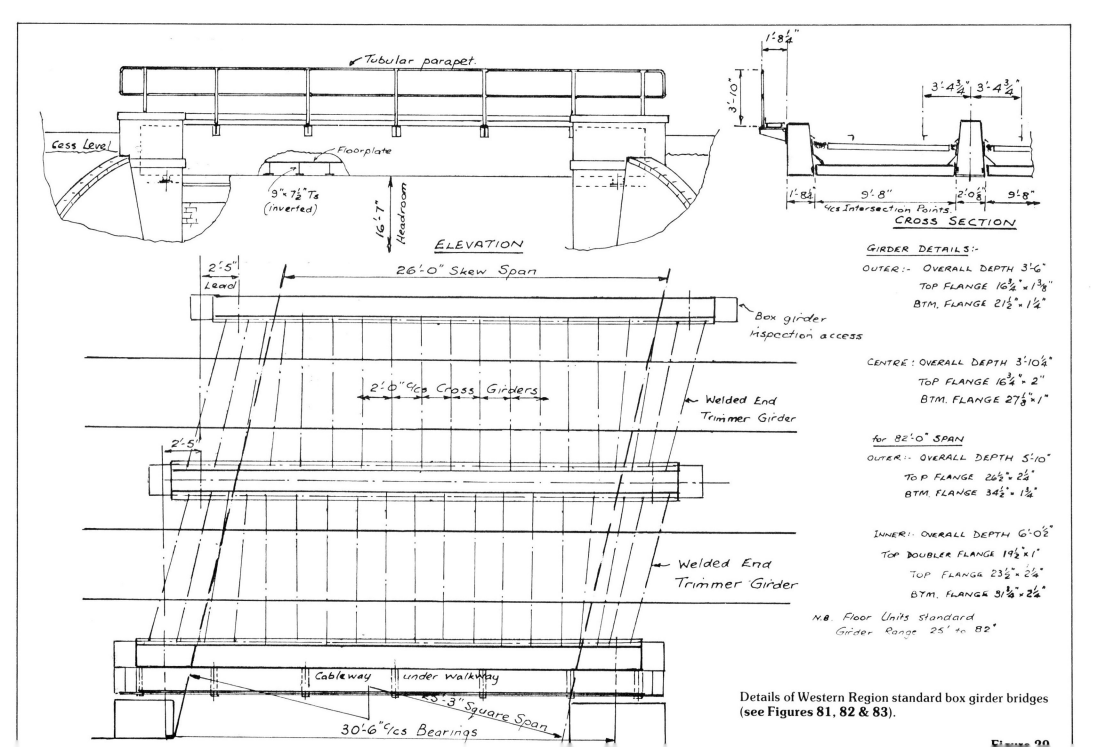

Tubular parapet.

Cess Level

Floorplate

9" × 7½" Ts (inverted)

16'-7" Headroom

ELEVATION

1'-8¼"

3'-10"

3'-4¾" | 3'-4¾"

1'-8¼"   9'-8"   2'-0⅞"   9'-8"

c/cs Intersection Points.

CROSS SECTION

GIRDER DETAILS:-

OUTER:- OVERALL DEPTH 3'-6"
TOP FLANGE 16¾" × 1⅜"
BTM. FLANGE 21½" × 1¼"

CENTRE: OVERALL DEPTH 3'-10¼"
TOP FLANGE 16¾" × 2"
BTM. FLANGE 27⅓" × 1"

for 82'-0" SPAN

OUTER:- OVERALL DEPTH 5'-10"
TOP FLANGE 26½" × 2¼"
BTM. FLANGE 34½" × 1¼"

INNER:- OVERALL DEPTH 6'-0½"
TOP DOUBLER FLANGE 19½" × 1"
TOP FLANGE 23½" × 2¼"
BTM. FLANGE 31¼" × 2¼"

N.B. Floor Units standard
Girder Range 25' to 82'

2'-5" Lead

26'-0" Skew Span

Box girder inspection access

2'-0" c/cs Cross Girders

Welded End Trimmer Girder

2'-5"

Welded End Trimmer Girder

Cableway   under walkway

25'-3" Square Span

30'-6" c/cs Bearings

Details of Western Region standard box girder bridges
(see Figures 81, 82 & 83).

Figure 20

Figure 30   An elliptical masonry arch near Kenilworth.

L. Wood

Figure 32

Connection (keying) of voussoir stones to a brick arch (masonry abutments below springing).

L. Wood

Figure 31

A multi-span elliptical arch viaduct, partly filled-in with brick diaphragm walls (note spandrel tie bars).

L. Wood

Figure 33 A three ring segmental brick arch with an ornamental parapet, near Sheffield Park on the Bluebell Railway. Note the minimum headroom signs.

Figure 34

A masonry pier of an elliptical arch viaduct. Note the ties to stop bulging spandrels.

L. Wood

Figure 35

A typical arch viaduct, with spans enclosed and let out as tenancies. Note the cantilever safety refuges and ornamental corbelled brickwork (near Leeds).

L. Wood

Figure 36

A four ring segmental brick arch with panelled parapet brickwork (near Barrow-in-Furness).

British Rail

Figure 37

A five segmental brick viaduct. Note the drainage from the spandrels (near Buckingham, ex-LNWR).

L. Wood

Figure 38

A seven ring segmental brick arch, again with panelled parapet, over a canal. A new reinforced concrete road bridge, with tubular steel parapet, is in the background (near Nottingham Victoria ex-GCR). Panelled brickwork was a distinctive feature of GCR construction (the arch was built in the late 1890s).

L. Wood

Figure 39

A semi-circular masonry arch. Note the shaping of the voussior stones and the dressed finish to the stones (note that the bridge has been widened on the far side with metallic portion).

L. Wood

Figure 40

A builder's plate on a cast-iron arch bridge. Note the shaped masonry springing course (Radcliffe Viaduct near Nottingham, ex-GNR).

L. Wood

Figure 41 A cast-iron arch, with castellated pier and pilaster, built in 1850 (near Manchester (Deansgate), ex-MSJA).

L. Wood

Figure 43 A castellated brick and masonry pier. Note the different forms of spandrel bracing and parapets on the adjacent bridge. The MSJA had distinctive bridge numberplates — oval with the letters MSJAR in the rim. Both the Cheshire Lines Committee and the Great Northern Railway constructed similar cast-iron arches around Manchester (Central), Deansgate warehouse (GNR).

L. Wood

Figure 42 A cast-iron arch, showing the site joint in castings and diaphragms between ribs.

L. Wood

Figure 44

A cast-iron arch with ornamental spandrels and parapet, extended in timber
boarding (near Manchester, ex-MSJA) and built in 1850.

British Rail

Figure 45 A cast-iron arch, showing widening of ribs at site joints. Note the track carrying beams are of a much heavier section than those under the parapet portion
(between Oxford Road and Deansgate Stations; BR glass fibre numberplate).

British Rail

Figure 46

A cast-iron edge beam bridge with the open type parapet (near Atherstone ex-LNWR).

British Rail

Figure 47

An inside view of a cast-iron parapet. Note the stiffening ribs and bolted connections.

British Rail

Figure 48 A multiple span wrought-iron viaduct, with an ornamental cast-iron spandrel bracing, string course and parapet. Note the line of the string course is reproduced in the masonry at the pier (River Thames bridge near Battersea, West London Extension Line, built in 1863).

British Rail

Figure 50

A close up of spandrel bracing. Note the difference between the ornamental cast iron work to the outer girder, and wrought-iron connections to the inner girder. Note also the diaphragm plates between the pairs of girders.

British Rail

Figure 51

An interior view, showing wrought-iron spandrel bracing and internal diagonal tie bars. Note the cross girders with dished floor plates and drainage outlets.

British Rail

Figure 52

A view on top of the bridge, during redecking. The original deck is on the left-hand side of the cross girders, with dished floor plate and longitudinal rail timbers, whilst the new deck consists of pressed-steel troughing with ballasted cross sleeper track.

British Rail

Figure 53 A wrought-iron longitudinal trough girder bridge, beneath the track, with a cast-iron parapet beam, timber decking and parapet. Note the retaining straps to the longitudinal timber, and also the sprinkling of ballast within

Figure 55

A typical cast-iron parapet beam of a bridge fitted with a tubular handrail, partly missing. These handrails were standard LNWR features for small span bridges (ex-LNWR bridge, near Leighton Buzzard).

L. Wood

Figure 54

A longer span hog-backed wrought-iron longitudinal trough girder and dished floor plate bridge. Again, the top of the cast-iron parapet beam is visible, and the pipe carries a telephone cable (ex-MR bridge, near Asfordby) — **for details see Figure 19**.

L. Wood

Figure 56

An interesting view on a closed line, with the timber deck removed, showing longitudinal timbers notched over cross girders, stiffeners connected to the tops of the cross girders, with transoms and transom bolts and steel cover plates to splice (ex-LNWR bridge on the Dunstable branch).

L. Wood

Figure 57

Another view showing riveted curved top flange plates stiffened by a longitudinal edge angle. Note the rivets staggered through a stiffener angle and the bottom flange angles.

L. Wood

Figure 58

Cast-iron beams under sidings with a timber deck. Note the difference between top and bottom flanges, the fillets to stiffeners and the flange to web connections. This type of construction was familiar in many parts of the country, and particularly in instances where additional low capacity lines such as sidings were required.

Author's Collection

Figure 59 (Below, top left): A steel underbridge of unusual construction with main girders, cross girders and rail bearers, with troughing connected off the top flanges of cross girders and supported by the rail bearers. Note the enamelled face bricks to the abutments and the cast-iron parapet (bridge near Mauldeth Road, Styal line, built 1908). Although of unusual construction, this style was repeated many times on 'turn of the century' LNWR lines, and was also used extensively on MSLR/GCR lines.

R. L. Murton

Figure 61 (Below, bottom left): An ornamental cast-iron parapet and pilaster, and infill to the outer girder. It is a normal two track, three girder bridge, with cross girders and rail bearers (Abbey Foregate Bridge, Shrewsbury).

L. Wood

Figure 60

(Below, top right): A view on top, showing cross-timbered track sitting in troughs and carried through to support a timber walkway.

R. L. Murton

Figure 62

(Below, bottom right): A narrow and low underbridge, with steel girders with concrete slab deck units, concrete-faced abutment and wingwalls. To allow for wider carriageways, a pedestrian subway is provided to the right (ex-London Transport bridge near Great Missenden, built 1948, subway added 1973).

L. Wood

Figure 64

A cast-iron trestle with wrought-iron bracing, wrought-iron girders and early trough decking, timber ballast boards (ex-MR bridge, near Bennerley).

L. Wood

Figure 65

A wrought-iron deck span type bridge with hog-backed parapet girders and timber deck. Note the shaped noses on the masonry piers, the new reinforced concrete piles to support the new superstructure, and the crosshead beam to piles already cast in the second span (near Floriston, ex-CR).

British Rail

Figure 66

A three girder steel bridge with transverse pressed-steel troughing, and cantilevered walkway with open type parapet (ex-GW/GC Joint line near Saunderton, built 1898). The Great Central also often used transverse troughing.

L. Wood

Figure 67

A longitudinal pressed-steel troughing bridge (ex-GW/GC Joint line, near Bradenham, built 1898). This type of bridge was also used extensively by the GWR on the Bala to Festiniog line.

L. Wood

Figure 68 A three girder steel bridge and, in the distance, a two girder bridge. Note the different parapets on the adjacent bridges (ex-GNR bridges, near Nottingham, built 1899).

British Rail

Figure 69 (Below): A three girder steel bridge. Note, on centre girder, the additional flange plates and timber ballast boards (ex-GCR bridge on the main line south of Nottingham at Weekday Cross Junction, built 1899).

British Rail

Figure 70

The outer girder of a three girder bridge. Note the refuge in the pilaster and GCR bridge numberplate.

Author's Collection

Figure 71

A deck span warren truss girder bridge, with lattice parapet (ex-GNR bridge, near Nottingham, built 1899).

L. Wood

Figure 72

A hog-backed girder bridge. Note that the sections of the diagonals vary in thickness, and also different girder details to suit the tapered span (ex-GCR main line bridge, near Nottingham, built 1899).

British Rail

Figure 73

A close up showing the open section bottom booms, underslung cross girders, rail bearers and floor plating, including the stiffened ballast plate upstand. Note also the pedestal type bearing on the nearside girder.

British Rail

Figure 74

A view of the skew end, showing short cross girders and rail bearers bearing on the abutment, stiffening ties to the floorplate, and braced outriggers to the main vertical members.

British Rail

(Above): A view of a warren truss girder bridge, of which the bottom boom has been strengthened by three high tensile bars, post-tensioned on the outside. Note the smoke plates to protect steelwork from engine blast (ex-GCR Intersection bridge at Nottingham Midland).

British Rail

An overhead lattice bracing to a hog-backed girder bridge. Note the guard rails in case of derailment, the brick upstand to the ballast plate to prevent corrosion, and the individual smoke plates to the members (ex-GCR bridge, near Nottingham Victoria).

Author's Collection

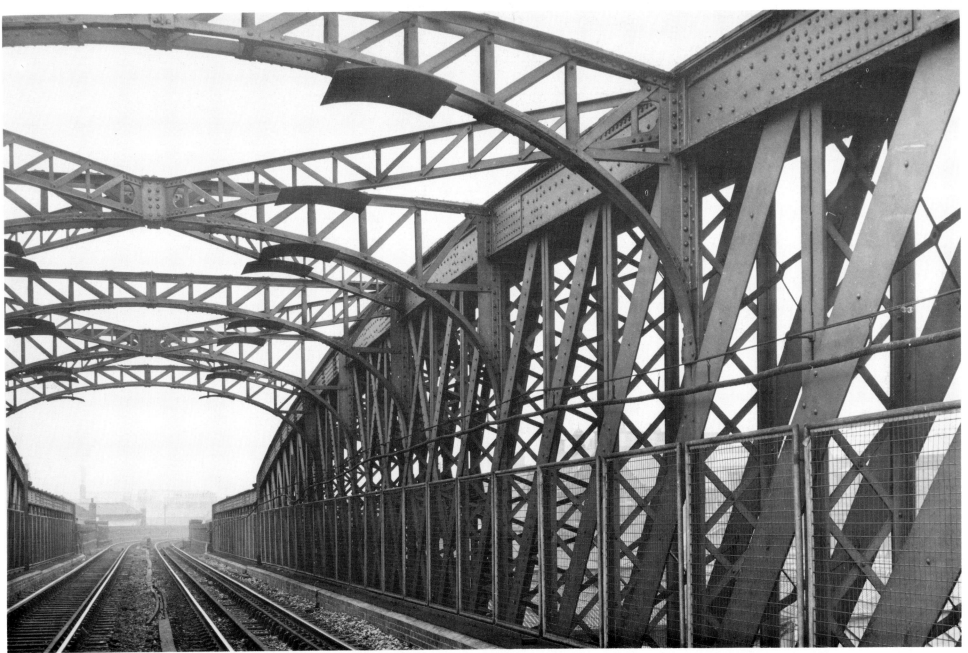

Figure 77

A standard British Rail type 'A' underbridge (near Leeds City).

L. Wood

Figure 78

A colliery branch underbridge, where piles have been used as columns to support reinforced concrete spans (near Rectory Junction, ex-GNR, built 1960).

L. Wood

Figure 79

A standard British Rail pre-stressed concrete rectangular beam bridge with a reinforced parapet beam. Note the up-stand on the bedcourse to support this unit (ex-GW&GC Joint line, near Princes Risborough, built 1970).

L. Wood

Figure 80

A reinforced concrete box culvert and wing walls cast in situ and constructed in 1982. Note the drainage spigots from the bottom of the wing walls.

L. Wood

Figure 81

A box girder bridge in its final position. Note the culvert through the back of the abutment for the roadside ditch, and the very tidy and pleasing elevation.

British Rail

Figure 82

An interesting view of a four track box girder bridge, ready for rolling into position and supported on military trestling. Note the fanning of the cross girders to suit the skew (near Atherstone, ex-LNWR).

British Rail

Figure 83

A track view of the same bridge. Note the signal and telephone cables ducted beneath the walkway on the right-hand side. Also note the British Rail oval bridge plate.

British Rail

Figure 84

If one won't do — segmental masonry arch with an overlaid five ring brick arch. Track has been raised to form a flyover instead of a flat junction. Note the loading is still brought down the line of the original columns (at Proof House Junction, Birmingham).

L. Wood

Overbridges

In the early days of railways, with track speeds generally low, it was customary for all roads and paths to cross the railway on the level (i.e. by constructing level crossings). As speeds increased, safety requirements became more stringent, and overbridges were more often built over the railway when on reasonably level ground, as to construct an underbridge with sufficient headroom would probably have involved the provision of a pumped drainage scheme as water would gather within the 'dip'.

As one travels along the various lines built by the pre-grouping companies, it is fairly obvious that, as far as overbridges are concerned, each company had its standard designs. Many Midland Railway, Great Northern and Great Western three span arch bridges exist where the centre span crosses the track, whilst the two side spans sit on bank seats.

Similarly, the LNWR have their familiar box girder overbridges over most of the four track section between London and Crewe.

Many cast-iron overbridges still exist, namely on the accommodation and occupation type structures, and some with weight restrictions.

Whilst many wrought-iron or steel bridges still exist, many have been reconstructed in pre-stressed concrete as a result of electrification schemes or other local authority road widening requirements. Even with the protection of smoke plates, these metallic overbridges suffered from steam engine blast. The sulphur deposits lead to corrosion causing a loss of section and overstressing the structure, making reconstruction essential.

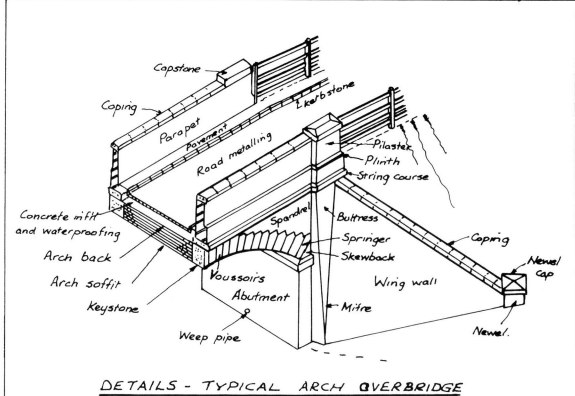

DETAILS - TYPICAL ARCH OVERBRIDGE

Masonry overbridge near Carnforth on the Lancaster & Carlisle main line.

British Rail

This shows a masonry arch with brick infill arches between voussoir stones. It is suitable for spans up to 50ft.

Figure 85

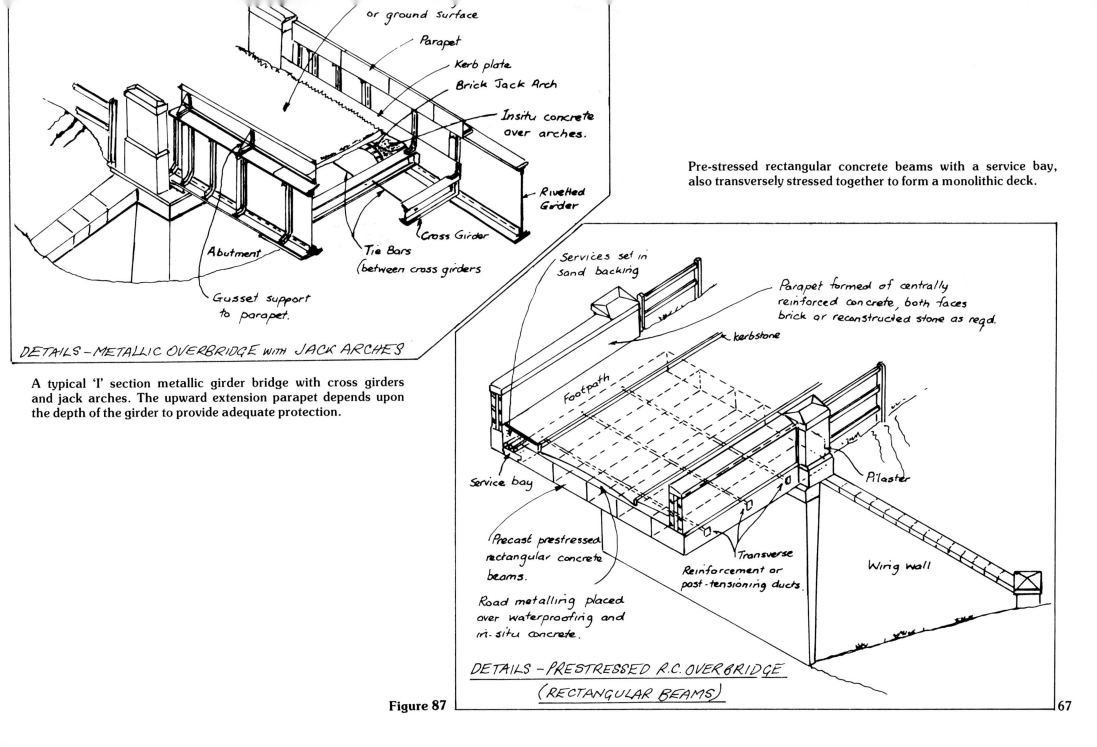

or ground surface

Parapet

Kerb plate

Brick Jack Arch

Insitu concrete over arches.

Riveted Girder

Cross Girder

Tie Bars (between cross girders

Abutment

Gusset support to parapet.

DETAILS – METALLIC OVERBRIDGE WITH JACK ARCHES

A typical 'I' section metallic girder bridge with cross girders and jack arches. The upward extension parapet depends upon the depth of the girder to provide adequate protection.

Pre-stressed rectangular concrete beams with a service bay, also transversely stressed together to form a monolithic deck.

Services set in sand backing

Parapet formed of centrally reinforced concrete, both faces brick or reconstructed stone as reqd.

kerbstone

Footpath

Service bay

Pilaster

Precast prestressed rectangular concrete beams.

Transverse Reinforcement or post-tensioning ducts.

Wing wall

Road metalling placed over waterproofing and in-situ concrete.

DETAILS – PRESTRESSED R.C. OVERBRIDGE (RECTANGULAR BEAMS)

Figure 87

67

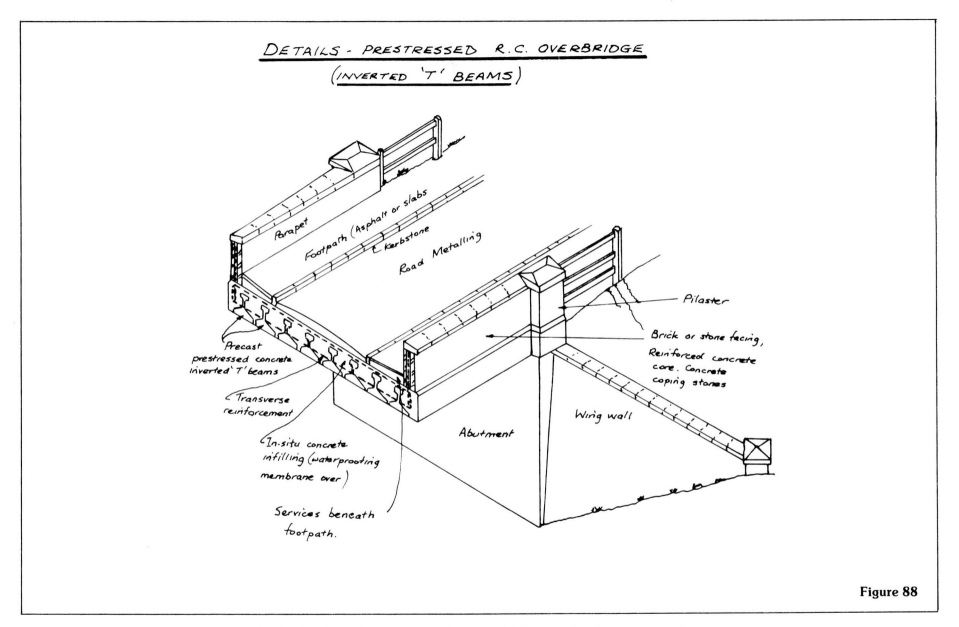

DETAILS - PRESTRESSED R.C. OVERBRIDGE
(INVERTED 'T' BEAMS)

Parapet

Footpath (Asphalt or slabs

← Kerbstone

Road Metalling

Pilaster

Precast prestressed concrete inverted 'T' beams

← Transverse reinforcement

← In-situ concrete infilling (waterproofing membrane over)

Services beneath footpath.

Brick or stone facing, Reinforced concrete core. Concrete coping stones

Wing wall

Abutment

Figure 88

A similar bridge, but using pre-stressed inverted 'T' beams. Services are carried beneath the pavements. These beams are not stressed together, but reinforcement is placed through the beams to bond the in situ concrete into place.

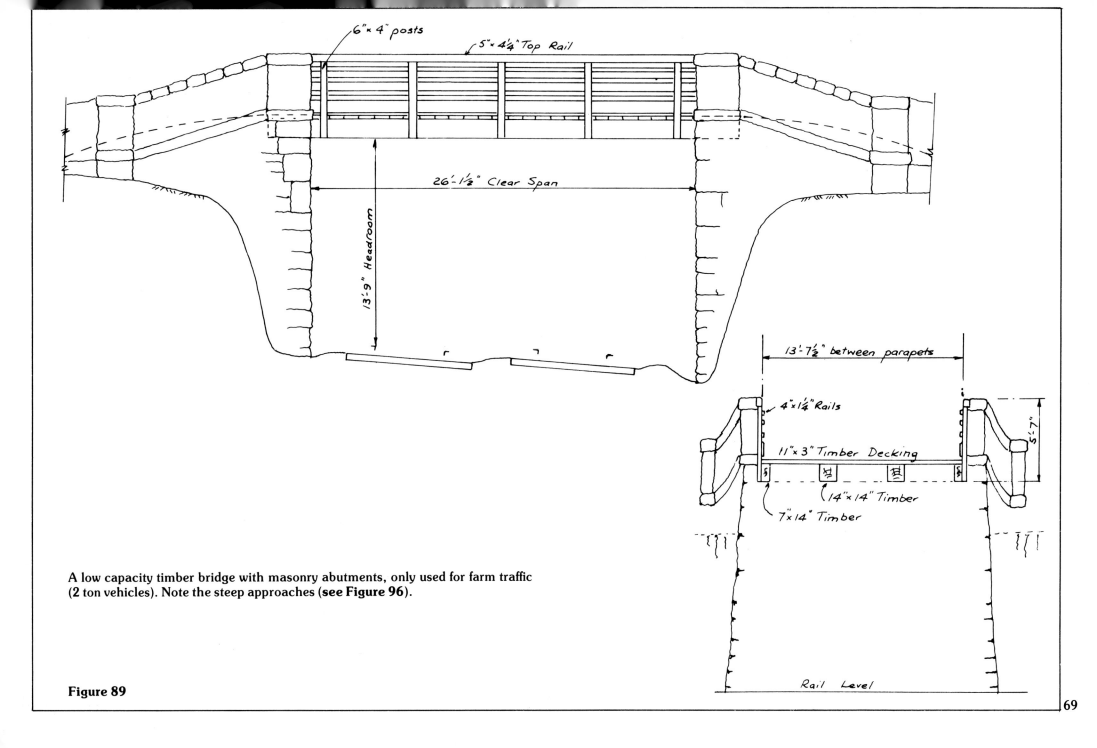

6"× 4" posts

5"× 4¼" Top Rail

26'-1½" Clear Span

13'-9" Headroom

13'-7½" between parapets

4"×1¼" Rails

5'-7"

11"× 3" Timber Decking

14"×14" Timber

7"×14" Timber

Rail Level

A low capacity timber bridge with masonry abutments, only used for farm traffic (2 ton vehicles). Note the steep approaches (**see Figure 96**).

Figure 89

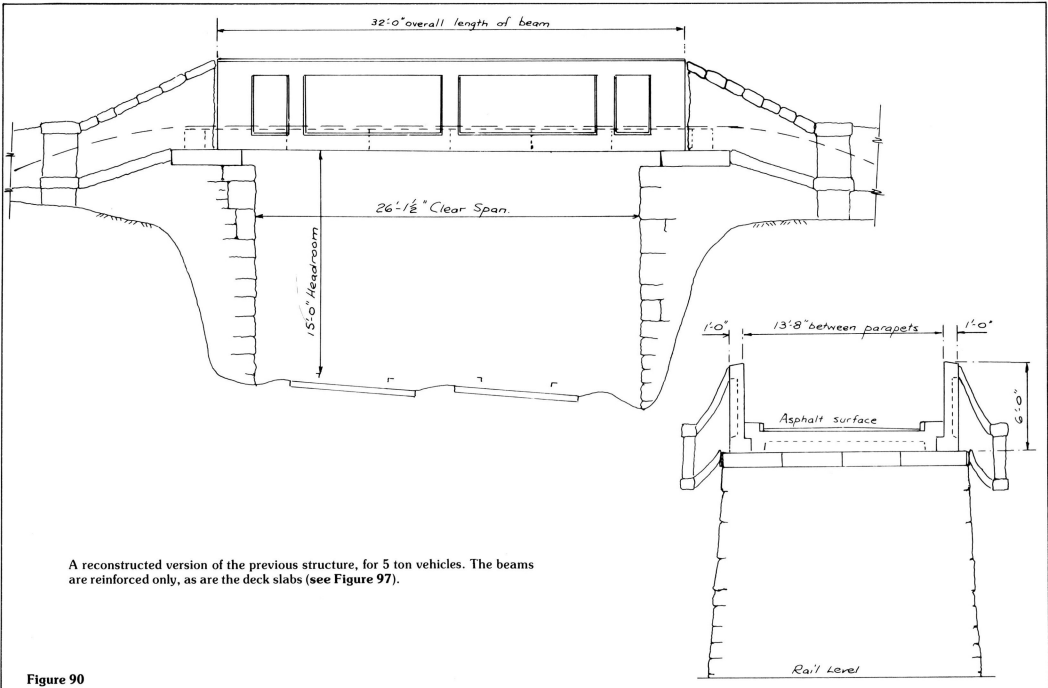

32'-0" overall length of beam

26'-1½" Clear Span.

15'-0" Headroom

1'-0" 13'-8" between parapets 1'-0"

6'-0"

Asphalt surface

Rail Level

A reconstructed version of the previous structure, for 5 ton vehicles. The beams are reinforced only, as are the deck slabs (**see Figure 97**).

Figure 90

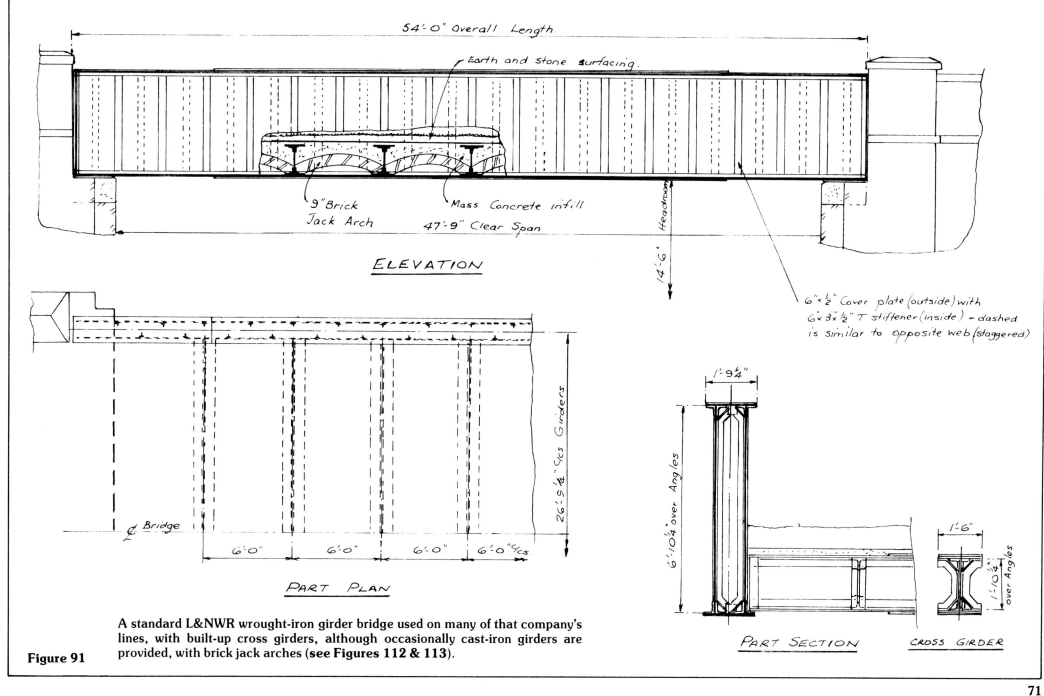

54'-0" Overall Length.

Earth and stone surfacing.

9" Brick Jack Arch

Mass Concrete infill

47'-9" Clear Span

14'-6" Headroom

ELEVATION

6"×½" Cover plate (outside) with
6×3×½" T stiffener (inside) - dashed
is similar to opposite web (staggered)

26'-9¼" C/cs Girders

₵ Bridge

6'-0" 6'-0" 6'-0" 6'-0" C/cs.

PART PLAN

1'-9¼"

6'-10¼" over Angles

1'-10¼" over Angles

PART SECTION

1'-6"

1'-10¼" over Angles

CROSS GIRDER

A standard L&NWR wrought-iron girder bridge used on many of that company's lines, with built-up cross girders, although occasionally cast-iron girders are provided, with brick jack arches (see Figures 112 & 113).

Figure 91

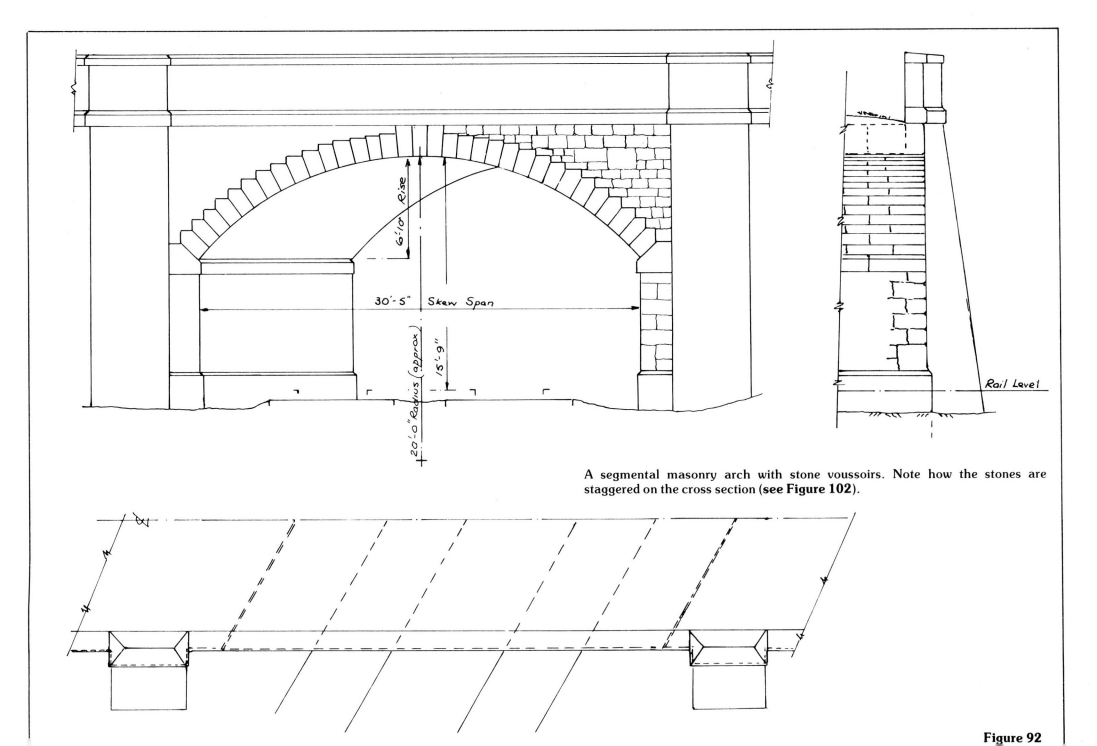

6'·10" Rise

30'-5" Skew Span

20'-0" Radius (approx)

15'-9"

Rail Level

A segmental masonry arch with stone voussoirs. Note how the stones are staggered on the cross section (see **Figure 102**).

Figure 92

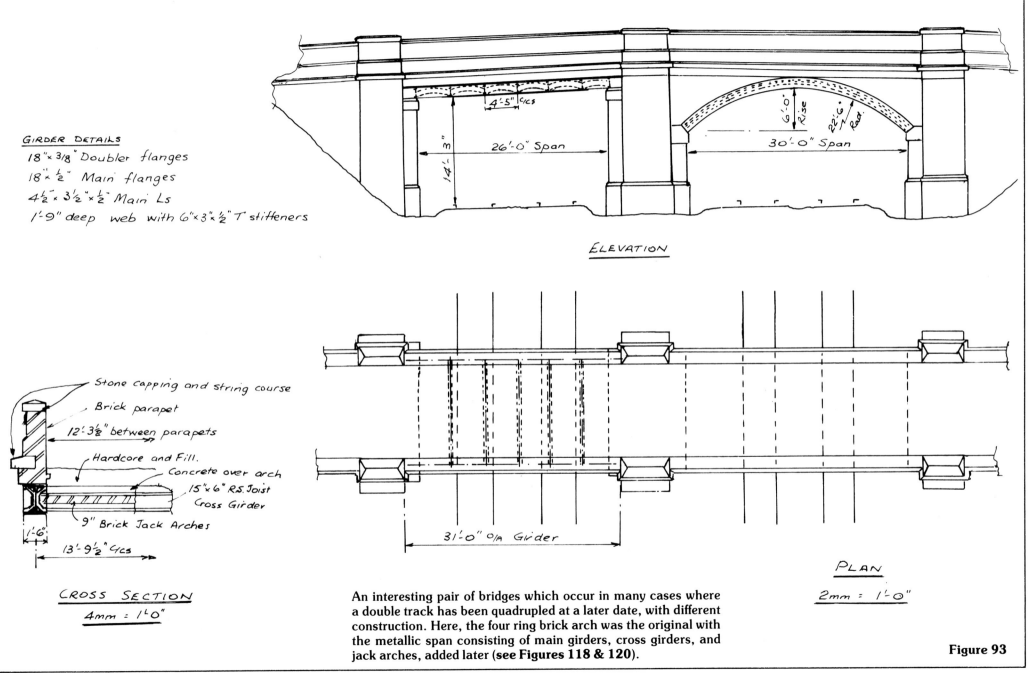

GIRDER DETAILS
18" x 3/8" Doubler flanges
18" x 1/2" Main flanges
4 1/2" x 3 1/2" x 1/2" Main Ls
1'-9" deep web with 6" x 3" x 1/2" T stiffeners

4'-5" c/cs

6'-0" Rise

22'-6" Rad

26'-0" Span

30'-0" Span

14'-3"

ELEVATION

Stone capping and string course

Brick parapet

12'-3 1/2" between parapets

Hardcore and Fill.

Concrete over arch

15" x 6" R.S. Joist Cross Girder

9" Brick Jack Arches

1'-6"

13'-9 1/2" c/cs

CROSS SECTION
4mm = 1'-0"

31'-0" O/A Girder

PLAN
2mm = 1'-0"

An interesting pair of bridges which occur in many cases where a double track has been quadrupled at a later date, with different construction. Here, the four ring brick arch was the original with the metallic span consisting of main girders, cross girders, and jack arches, added later (**see Figures 118 & 120**).

Figure 93

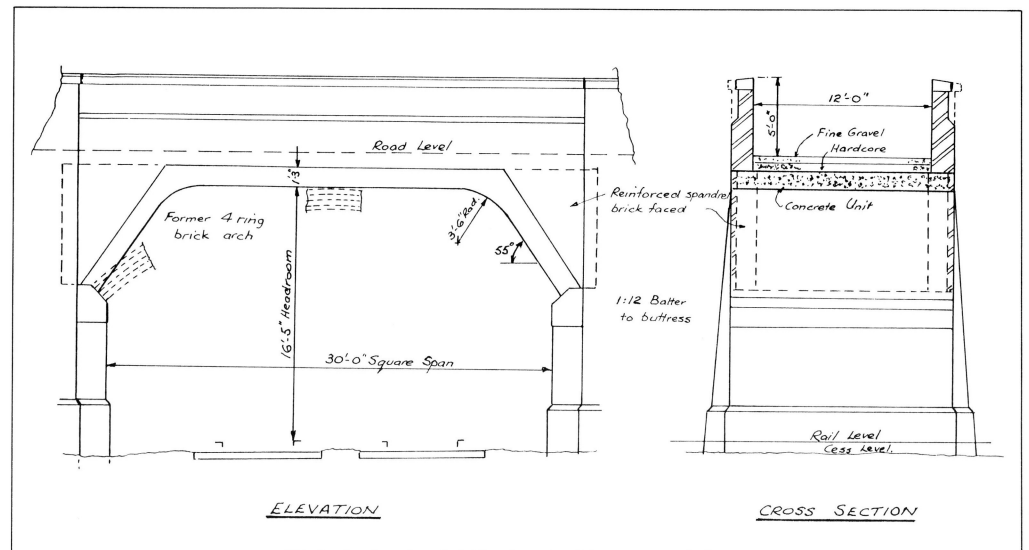

ELEVATION

CROSS SECTION

Road Level

1'3"

Former 4 ring brick arch

16'-5" Headroom

3'-6" Rad.

55°

30'-0" Square Span

Reinforced spandrel brick faced

1:12 Batter to buttress

12'-0"

5'-0"

Fine Gravel Hardcore

Concrete Unit

Rail Level
Cess Level.

This drawing shows how the brick arch portion of the previous overbridge was reconstructed to give clearance for overhead electrification. The parapet and spandrels are removed, and parts of the arch ring and the remaining portion is used to support the shuttering to form the portal arch. In some cases this was not possible and pre-cast arch units were used instead (see Figure 129). The metallic span was jacked up and positioned on new bearing grillages to increase the headroom for that portion (see Figure 119).

Figure 94

A standard inverted 'T' beam bridge with a service bay beneath the pavement. For larger spans, the widths of the beams are identical, but the depth is increased.

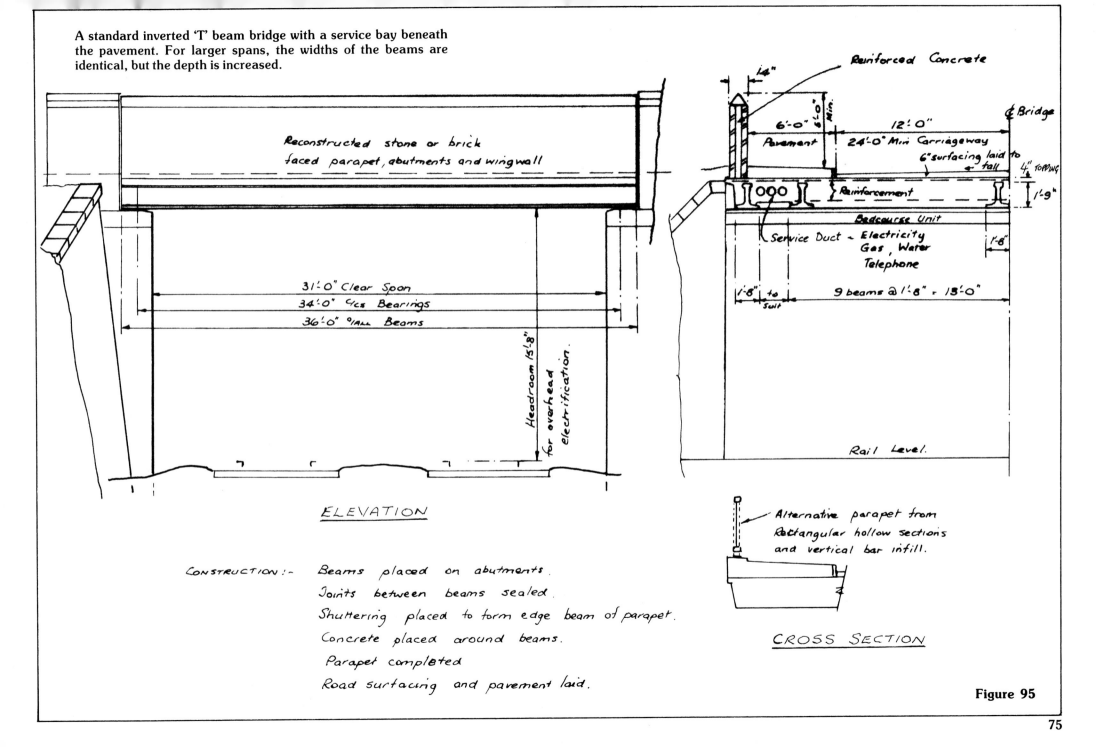

Reinforced Concrete

14"

6'-0"

6'-0" Min.

12'-0"

℄ Bridge

Pavement

24'-0" Mini Carriageway

6" surfacing laid to fall

4¼" Topping

Reinforcement

1'-9"

Bedcourse Unit

Service Duct - Electricity Gas, Water Telephone

1'-8"

Reconstructed stone or brick faced parapet, abutments and wingwall

31'-0" Clear Span

34'-0" C/cs Bearings

36'-0" O/ALL Beams

Headroom 15'-8" for overhead electrification.

1'-8" to suit

9 beams @ 1'-8" = 15'-0"

Rail Level.

ELEVATION

CONSTRUCTION:- Beams placed on abutments.
Joints between beams sealed.
Shuttering placed to form edge beam of parapet.
Concrete placed around beams.
Parapet completed
Road surfacing and pavement laid.

Alternative parapet from Rectangular hollow sections and vertical bar infill.

CROSS SECTION

Figure 95

Figure 96

A timber overbridge with masonry abutments (near Cark & Cartmel, ex-Furness Railway).

Author's Collection

Figure 97

A reinforced concrete beam bridge with a slab deck. Note the steel smoke plates. This bridge is situated on the ex-Furness railway line from Carnforth to Whitehaven and was reconstructed in 1953. Bridges were numbered from Carnforth and the bridge number plate can be seen on the left.

British Rail

Figure 98 A very early view of the erection of a cast-iron arch bridge. It is a segmental arch which is constructed with three bolted sections (circa 1890-92), and is situated on the approaches to Leicester (London Road).

Author's Collection

Figure 99 Unusual wrought-iron segmental arch rings with voussoir stones above the ring. Note the ornamental string course (near Coventry). This is probably a Stephenson original.

British Rail

Figure 100 An interesting elliptical masonry arch with extended voussoir stones. Note the prominent keystone and the bridge numberplate which was the standard type for the LNWR/LMS/BR. The bridge is situated between Weaver Junction and Walton Junction. The radiating voussoirs were a well-known feature, particularly on lines built by Joseph Locke.

British Rail

Figure 101

A five brick ring three span arch in a deep sandstone cutting. These arches, having brick rings and stone spandrels, were quite widespread, particularly in the Peak District, on both LNWR and MR lines. The brick parapets above a string course have been rebuilt following mining subsidence (near Southwell, ex-Midland Railway).

British Rail

Figure 102 A two span segmental masonry arch structure (near Mansfield, ex-Midland Railway).

British Rail

Figure 103

An elliptical masonry arch which has been widened on the far side by a reinforced concrete beam construction. The parapet was probably reconstructed at this time (at Cross Gates, near Leeds, ex-North Eastern Railway).

L. Wood

Figure 104

A segmental masonry arch, many of which were found on the Chester to Holyhead line. Note the curved string course to suit the road surface profile, and also the two other adjacent identical bridges (near Flint ex-LNWR).

L. Wood

Figure 105

A flat segmental masonry arch incorporating platforms within the span (at Delamere, on the Altrincham to Chester line, ex-Cheshire Lines Committee).

L. Wood

Figure 106

A cast-iron edge beam bridge to wrought-iron longitudinal girders with jackarches (near Bedford St. Johns, ex-LNWR).

L. Wood

Figure 107 (Right):

Following the 'Bridgeguard' exercise from 1964, this was a fairly common sight around the country, showing propped spans where no tracks now exist. This is a cast-iron edge beam bridge with an ornamental masonry string course and facing to the pier (Brook Street Bridge, Chester, ex-LNWR).

L. Wood

Figure 109 (Lower right):

A view on top of the same bridge.

L. Wood

Figure 108 (Below):

Two four ring brick arches, slightly skewed. Both arches had a single track passing through (at Roade, ex-SMJ line).

L. Wood

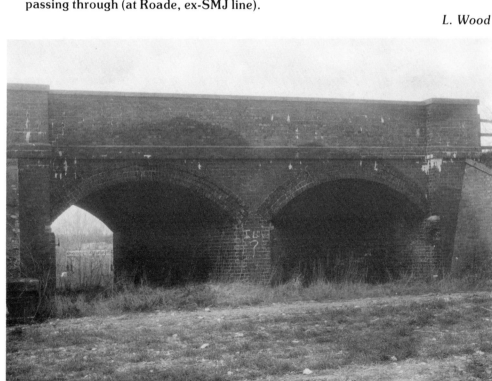

Figure 110 A view of an ex-GWR four ring elliptical brick arch bridge, built in 1869, with a curved masonry string course (at Wilmcote). The bridge number plate is a BR addition.

British Rail

Figure 111

A metallic bridge on a considerable gradient. The top of the girder is made horizontal for bearing (under the nearside corner of the masonry pilaster). It was situated near Teignmouth, ex-GWR.

L. Wood

Figure 112

A wrought-iron box girder bridge, of an almost standard LNWR type. Note that there are no external stiffeners, only cover plates (near Hanslope, ex-LNWR) — **for details see Figure 91**.

British Rail

Figure 113

A top view of the same bridge. Note the manholes, to enable the interior of the girder bridge to be examined and maintained. The bridge is used only by the farmer (occupation) and hence has an unmade road surface.

British Rail

Figure 114

Another occupation bridge, which has just been raised for an electrification scheme. The ends of the girders are visible, as are the two ring jack arches, overlaid with about three inches of concrete (near Styal, ex-LNWR).

British Rail

Figure 115

Attachments to an overbridge, with anti-trespass wires to the top flange and walkways to suspended signals off the bottom flange (at the old Coventry Station).

Author's Collection

Figure 116

A view on the top showing Loughborough Station entrance. Note the ornamental brickwork to the inside of the parapet. The GCR made the most of entrances to/from bridges on to island platforms.

British Rail

Figure 117 Station buildings adjacent to an overbridge. Note the shaped pilaster stones and the ex-GCR bridge numberplate (at Loughborough ex-GCR).

British Rail

Figure 118

Apparent on many lines which have been built as double track and then quad-rupled, two different forms of construction appear, the original arch and the later metallic span (longitudinal girders with jack arches). Note the string course well above the top of the girder, which is unusual, and the smoke plates under the metallic span (near Nuneaton, ex-LNWR) — **for details see Figures 93 & 94.**

British Rail

Figure 119

A view of the same bridge from the other face, after electrification. The metallic span has been raised. Note the new cill beams under the bearings and the arch portion replaced by a reinforced concrete portal. These were shuttered off the original arch, and then, after the concrete has cured, the brick arch is demolished by explosive from underneath.

British Rail

Figure 120 Another view across the top before raising. The coping in the parapet would not be allowed with overhead

Figure 121

A 12in. diameter water main, suspended off a reinforced concrete parapet beam. Note the quoined masonry corner of the abutment.

L. Wood

Figure 122

To ease the corner of a road junction, this bridge has been widened with an additional beam with a concrete slab cast over the top. Note the curve of the parapet wall (Brook Street Bridge, Chester).

L. Wood

Figure 123
Two bridges with different parapets supported off the trestle at the centre. It has deep flange angles with two rows of rivets (at King's Cross, Midland).

British Rail

Figure 124
A warren pattern girder bridge, also carrying a large diameter water pipe (near Gorton, ex-MS&LR). This is a former canal bridge, constructed by the GCR for the Ashburys to Hyde Junction widening, and built in 1905.

L. Wood

Figure 125
An inside view of the previous bridge, revealing a canal well, now partially filled

The bridge has been widened by extending abutments in concrete at the far side. A lattice girder footbridge has been placed in a temporary position to provide a pedestrian route whilst work is being carried out (near Preston Brook ex-LNWR).

British Rail

Figure 128

A view of a modern ring road, supported on heavy reinforced beams and columns, and the road superstructure was cast in situ. It is situated above the Chester to Holyhead line, near Northgate Street Tunnels, Chester.

L. Wood

Figure 129

A night scene, as reinforced concrete portal frames are placed on cill beams. A partially-demolished arch may be seen in the background (Kentish Town, ex-MR). This work was being carried out for the St. Pancras-Bedford Electrification Scheme in 1982.

British Rail

Footbridges

Station footbridges and other public footbridges were not provided in the early days of the railway, and hence very few wholly cast-iron structures exist, apart from those on ex-North Eastern Railway territory.

Timber footbridges do exist at a few locations but, more often, for relatively light construction, timber was used for the deck and the parapet and rolled- steel sections (braced together) were used for the main member. Some of these were provided with side glazing and a roof, whilst others were open to the elements. Most have a timber deck, although asphalt or other non-slip surface was also provided.

Later, footbridges were produced in an open lattice work riveted construction in wrought iron, which generally produced a relatively light but adequate structure. Usually, these bridges feature shaped outriggers to strengthen the top flanges which are weak in this form of construction.

Some of these bridges are provided with vertical board in-filling and again some are glazed and are also provided with roof covering.

Columns to many of these structures were of cast iron, often incorporating ornamental features. Both the London & North Western and Great Western railways had footbridges with cast-iron risers and parapets (see Figures 152 & 132 respectively) both of which were fitted with timber treads.

Later still, both wrought-iron and steel plate girders were provided, incorporating portal frames to support the glazing and the roof or alternatively incorporating outriggers to brace the top flanges.

More recently with the introduction of welding, footbridges have been produced with plate girders and also the various hollow sections (either square, rectangular or circular). This latter variety were introduced during the late 1950s and have been used by many local authorities to provide pedestrian walkways, enabling the carriageway to be widened without the expense of providing a complete new superstructure and associated substructure work.

Pre-cast and pre-stressed concrete footbridges are also used by the London Midland and Southern regions, and a few appear on ex-Great Western Railway lines. These often have feature panels incorporated, to produce a more attractive finish than the plain concrete (see Figures 134 & 135).

At many stations, the footbridge often doubles as a luggage bridge, whilst at others, separate structures are provided. Where such combined structures exist, a stronger deck is provided, sometimes with pressed steel or wrought-iron troughing or joists set within an in situ concrete deck. At these locations, staircases are provided for passengers whilst lifts are provided for the trolleys to be raised to deck level. Stations where combined but segregated facilities are provided include Nuneaton, Wrexham, Manchester (Piccadilly) and Bletchley. At other stations, separate luggage bridges are provided including Worcester (Shrub Hill) Exeter (St. David's) Coventry and Leicester. During the last fifteen years or so, The Post Office have had constructed fairly large metal-clad structures, similar to footbridges, which incorporate conveyors for handling mail. Examples may be seen at Bristol (Temple Meads), Preston, Stafford, and Manchester (Piccadilly). A further innovation during the past ten years or so has been the provision of stepped ramps in place of staircases, which gives elderly passengers, or those with perambulators, an easier ascent or descent. Many locations in the Liverpool and Manchester areas are receiving such ramps, although many ordinary ramps have existed on the Southern Region at Clapham, East Croydon and Waterloo (Eastern) for many years.

Figure 130

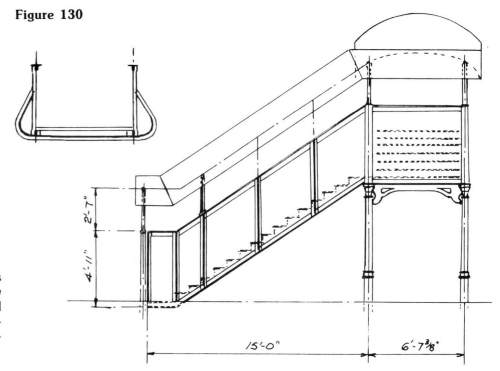

A Great Eastern plate girder footbridge with a corrugated sheeting roof. This footbridge was originally at Sudbury but has now been moved to the Stour Valley Railway at Chappel & Wakes Colne Station. The Great Eastern Railway had several bridges similar to this and also a lattice girder type of which many photographs appear in the Great Eastern books written by Dr Ian C. Allen and published by Oxford Publishing Co.

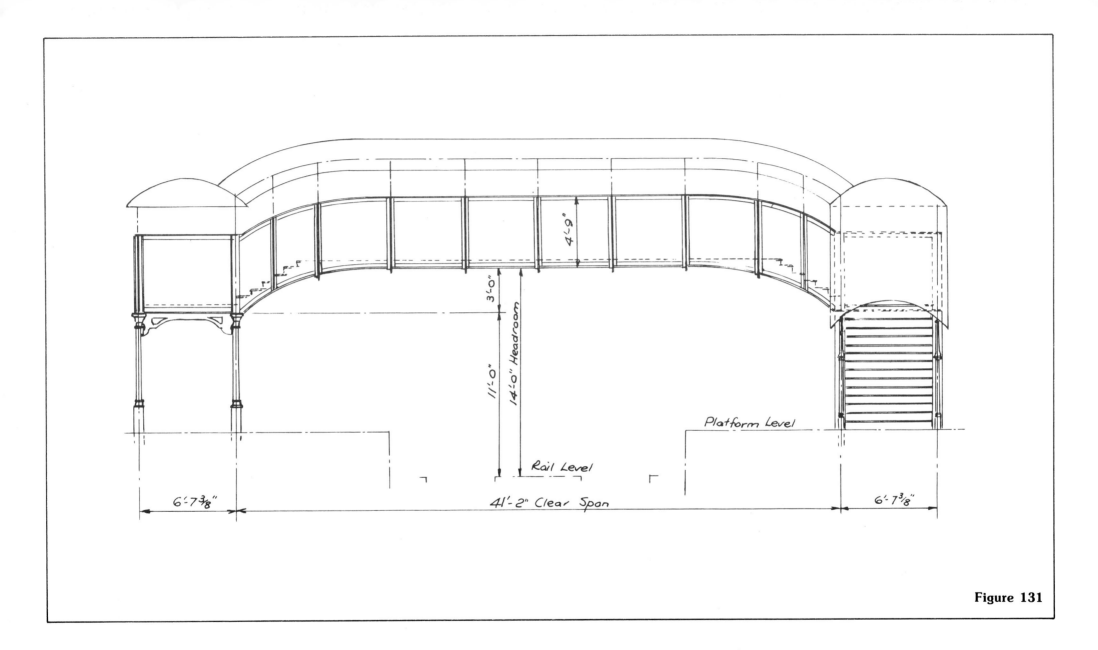

Figure 131

6'-7³⁄₈"

41'-2" Clear Span

6'-7³⁄₈"

Rail Level

Platform Level

14'-0" Headroom

11'-0"

3'-0"

4'-9"

A Great Western lattice girder footbridge with a corrugated sheeting roof (not always fitted). Outriggers are provided to strengthen the top flange of the lattice. Stair stringers are cast-iron mouldings to which the timber treads are fitted, together with a cast iron parapet. Other railways had very similar pattern footbridges (**see Figure 110**).

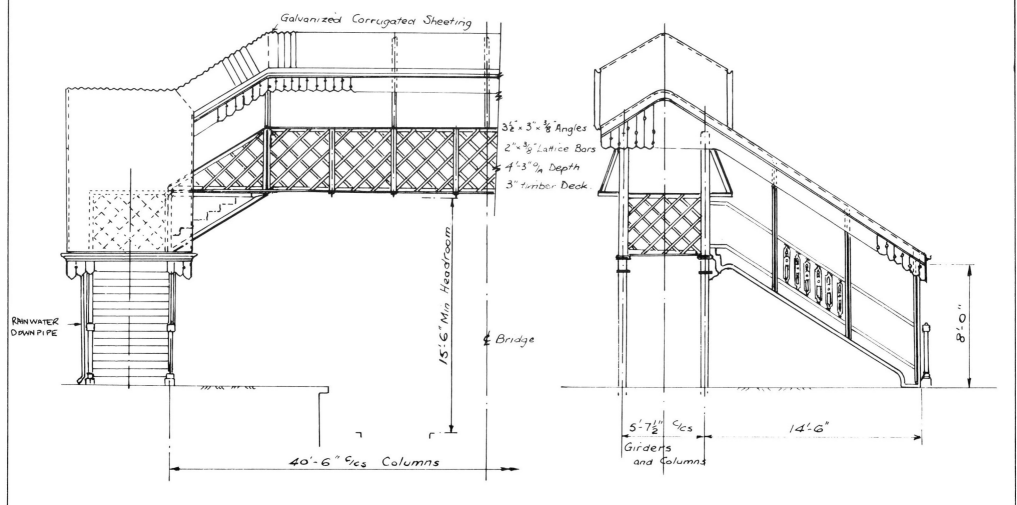

Galvanized Corrugated Sheeting

$3\frac{1}{2}" \times 3" \times \frac{3}{8}"$ Angles

$2" \times \frac{3}{8}"$ Lattice Bars

$4'$-$3"$ % Depth

$3"$ timber Deck.

RAINWATER DOWNPIPE

$15'$-$6"$ Min Headroom

₵ Bridge

$40'$-$6"$ ℀ₛ Columns

$5'$-$7\frac{1}{2}"$ ℀ₛ Girders and Columns

$14'$-$6"$

$8'$-$0"$

Figure 132

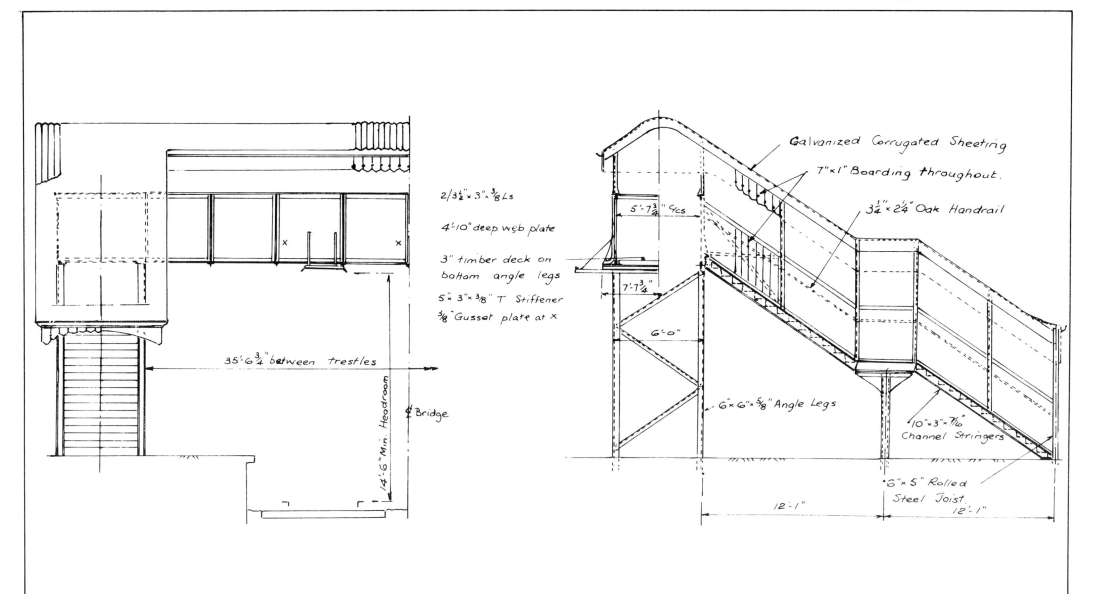

2/3½" × 3" × ⅜ Ls

4'-10" deep web plate

3" timber deck on
bottom angle legs

5" × 3" × ⅜" T Stiffener

⅜" Gusset plate at x

35'-6¾" between trestles

¢ Bridge

14'-6" Min. Headroom

Galvanized Corrugated Sheeting

7" × 1" Boarding throughout.

3¼" × 2¼" Oak Handrail

5'-7¾" c/cs

7'-7¾"

6'-0"

6" × 6" × ⅝" Angle Legs

10" × 3" × ⁷⁄₁₆" Channel Stringers

6" × 5" Rolled Steel Joist.

12'-1"

12'-1"

A Great Western plate girder footbridge with a corrugated sheeting roof. Top
flanges are stiffened by the portal frames to also support the roof. At some locations, side glazing is provided (see Figure 156).

Figure 133

Figure 134 An elevation of a modern post-tensioned footbridge with exposed aggregate feature panels. The reinforced concrete column support is fanned out to provide a landing, as well as to support the span and staircase (at Stechford, ex-LNWR, built 1965).

L. Wood

Figure 135 A side elevation of the staircase. Note the overhead tubular light fittings.

L. Wood

A modern pre-cast post-tensioned footbridge with exposed aggregate feature panels. The circular column is fanned out to provide a landing as well as providing support for the span and approach flight (**see Figures 134 & 135**).

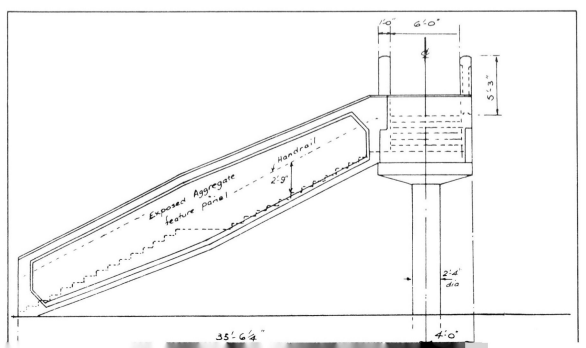

Figure 136 A timber footbridge spanning off a bank seat on the right-hand side (near Seascale, ex-Furness Railway). Again the standard Furness Railway numberplate is visible.

British Rail

Figure 137
A timber footbridge supported off two 18in. x 6in. rolled-steel joists with brick piers (near Gresford, ex-GWR).

L. Wood

Figure 138
A close up view of the timber parapet of the same bridge, showing the mesh infill.

L. Wood

Figure 139
A unique metallic segmental arch footbridge — also supporting a loading gauge

Figure 140
A timber-framed staircase, supported off brickwork, semi-glazed with a felt and timber roof. The station buildings are extended off the road overbridge (at

Figure 141

Wrought-iron underbridge girders, used for a footbridge, with timber parapets, approach staircases and masonry piers. This was the site of Fairfield Halt (ex-LNWR), looking towards Buxton. The sidings to the right are from Buxton Flying Junction.

British Rail

Figure 143

An aerial view of the bridge shown in **Figure 136**. Note the chamfering of the timber sections.

British Rail

Figure 142

A timber-clad semi-glazed station footbridge with an open lattice staircase. The staircase is sheeted and the bridge is situated at Guide Bridge (ex-MS&LR) and was built by the GCR, circa 1909.

L. Wood

Figure 144 A half-glazed lattice girder footbridge. Staircases would have been constructed within the station buildings in the bridge/masonry roof, from corrugated sheeting (at Banbury, ex-GWR). This view was photographed prior to the reconstruction of the station, circa 1956/7.

British Rail

Figure 145
A lattice girder staircase with timber treads and light trestles constructed from rolled-steel sections (at Royton East Junction, ex-L&Y Railway). Although typical of L&YR constructions, this bridge differed slightly from the standard design.

L. Wood

Figure 146
(**Above**): An inside view, showing the concrete deck and elliptical overhead bracing to strengthen the top flanges.

L. Wood

Figure 147
A lattice pattern footbridge with a graceful curve down to the trestles (which are not original, together with the new extension to right). Note the circular outriggers to strengthen the top flange (at Bennerley, ex-Midland Railway). This bridge has typical Midland Railway features.

Figure 148 A deeper lattice girder bridge, unusual as it has both outriggers and overhead bracing (at Cross Gates, ex-NER).

L. Wood

Figure 149 An open lattice footbridge with a timber deck and treads, used both for passengers and pedestrians (if gates were closed). Many examples similar to this exist throughout the country. Note the handrail carried across the span as well as on the stairs (at Congleton, ex-North Staffs Railway). This bridge, together with the level crossing, was removed in preparation for electrification.

Figure 150 A close up of the underside of the staircase at Congleton, showing the bracing to the span and the shaped outriggers, and the ornamental cast-iron columns.

Figure 153
The ornamental cast-iron columns and bracing to form the trestle for a lattice footbridge (at Doncaster, *ex*-GNR).

L. Wood

Figure 151 Two differing patterns of footbridge at the same location. The nearer is the station footbridge, whilst that at the platform end forms a public right of way but is not connected to the platform (at Flint, *ex*-LNWR). This footbridge was provided when the level crossing closed in the 1930s.

L. Wood

Figure 152 A close up of the station footbridge at Flint, showing cast-iron stringers and parapet with timber treads.

Figure 154
An open type of footbridge constructed from rolled section angles with timber deck and treads (at King's Cross, Midland City Line.

British Rail

Figure 155

A similar deeper open type warren girder bridge, made from angle, with mesh infill panels to approximately half height. Note the buttresses to the pier and timber approach span (at Aylesbury, ex-Metropolitan & GC Joint).

British Rail

Figure 156

A steel plate girder footbridge, formerly covered with a galvanised roof, but now only one support remains. It has a rolled-steel channel stringer to the stairs with a timber parapet (at Saunderton, ex-GW&GC Joint line).

L. Wood

Figure 157

An open lattice footbridge and stairs, with a timber deck. Note the five infill panels over the overhead electric wires. This bridge is situated at Gorton and was built by the GCR for the widening in 1904. It was shortened when the goods lines were taken out.

L. Wood

Figure 158

A plate girder footbridge, using a rolled-steel channel as a top flange for stiffness (near Smethwick, ex-LNWR).

British Rail

Figure 159

A close up of a three ring semi-arch forming a staircase for the same footbridge. Gas lighting and supply, and also other services, are carried across the footbridge. Note the shaped bricks to form capping to the stair parapets.

British Rail

Figure 160

A part of the walk around the city wall at Chester, showing the metallic girder bridge with masonry abutments, pier and parapets (ex-LNWR).

L. Wood

Figure 161

An inside view of the bridge. The tops of the girders are just visible above the concrete wearing surface.

L. Wood

Figure 162

A plate girder footbridge, half glazed and with a timber and felt roof, and with brick-built lift shafts (at Nuneaton, ex-LNWR). This bridge is typical of LNWR new works in the early 1900s, and similar to those in North Wales at Rhyl, Bangor, Llandudno Junction and Colwyn Bay.

L. Wood

Figure 163

An interior view showing segregated portions for luggage (left) and passengers (right).

L.Wood

Figure 164 A modern style steel-framed bridge with metal cladding for Post Office use (at Leeds).

Figure 165 A lightweight welded footbridge from 18in. x 6in. rolled-steel joists, with timber treads, framing a standard

Figure 166

A modern steel footbridge, formed from rectangular hollow sections with a reinforced concrete deck. Panels of mesh infill form the parapets. It is positioned for pedestrian use, to allow the narrow arch bridge to be used totally for road traffic. Note that the bridge is spaced away from the existing bridge to allow for the erection of scaffolding for maintenance purposes.

Author's Collection

Figure 167

Another view of the same bridge. The kerb has been left to protect the masonry parapet.

Author's Collection

Figure 168 Modern welded stepped ramp stairs, half-glazed with metal sheeting to the roof, at Birkenhead Park. There are

Figure 169 Ancient and modern — an old standard GWR lattice footbridge on the right together with a new reinforced concrete beam bridge, with a tubular parapet, on left-hand side (at Swan Village, ex-GWR).

British Rail

Figure 170

122

Culverts, Tunnels and others

In this section, in addition to tunnels and culverts, I have selected certain photographs of other details which may be of interest to modellers.

A six ring semicircular tunnel arch which has been cut through rock, and is well vegetated. Note the additional small three ring segmental arch, to

Figure 171

An elliptical brick arch tunnel. Nearer is a new construction of jack arch girders with precast jack arch units (near King's Cross, Midland City Line).

British Rail

Figure 172

A four ring brick arch horseshoe tunnel. The retaining wall formed part of a tunnel which was shortened following a partial collapse in the 1870s. Note the refuge in the immediate left-hand foreground (Preston Brook Tunnel, ex-LNWR).

L. Wood

Figure 173

A segmental masonry tunnel, with unusual shaped wing walls (Chorley Tunnel, ex-L&YR).

British Rail

Figure 174

Twin brick arch culverts, showing the usual problem of the build up of storm debris at the entrance (near Buckingham, ex-LNWR).

L. Wood

Figure 175

A new reinforced concrete box culvert with cast in situ headwalls (also near Buckingham).

L. Wood

Figure 176

New reinforced concrete box culvert units to provide a pedestrian subway, adjacent to a narrow road underbridge. It has cast in situ headwalls. Many of these subways were positioned by placing a steel shield in front of the concrete units, and jacking the whole assembly forward with miners working within the shield, removing the spoil. Rail traffic was usually subjected to a speed restriction whilst the work was in progress. Note the strengthening to lower portion of the wing wall (near Great Missenden, ex-Metropolitan Railway).

L. Wood

Figure 177

A close up of culvert units, showing the joints in the units. Lighting is usually incorporated in the chamfers at the top corners of the units.

L. Wood

Figure 178 A view of a subway unit being placed into position. The floor for the subway had already been laid (near Carpenders Park, ex-LNWR).

Figure 179
A semi-circular five ring brick arch. There is a trackside ditch outfall through the far wing wall. Note the fencing carried across the opening (near Golbourne, ex-LNWR).

L. Wood

Figure 180	Three 3ft. 6in. diameter pipes, conveying water to Liverpool. Note the decorative brickwork (Vyrnwy Aquaduct, near Delamere, ex-CLC).
	L. Wood
Figure 181	A view of the other abutment.
	L. Wood

Figure 182

Flood openings formed from rolled galvanized corrugated sheeting, with stone pitching to prevent erosion of the sides. These examples are near Loughborough, on the new link from the ex-Midland main line up to the ex-GCR line. Trains actually pass through a similar structure on the Middleton Railway in Leeds.

L. Wood

Figure 183

London Transport pattern cable bridges, formed in sections to an elliptical arch curve by rolling steel joist to the radius, with splices at approximately the quarter points of the span, at Farringdon, LT. Note LT structure number plate.

British Rail

Figure 184 Steelwork supporting a raft over the line for a warehouse. Riveted steel girders, with staggered rivets, are easily visible (near Barbican, on the Midland City Line).

British Rail

Figure 185

Positioning part of a long steel girder, fabricated in sections and spliced together when erected. A stiffener is located above the bearing which is already in position on top of the pier, adjacent to the top of the ladder, just visible. Note the four wheel girder wagon which has been used to transport the girder to the site (near West Hampstead, ex-MR). It was required to carry the North London line on its new alignment.

British Rail

Figure 186

Completing the far side girder of the same bridge. All the lower trackwork is timbered out to enable cranes and other plant to move about over the tracks as required.

British Rail

Figure 187

Twin 2ft. diameter service pipes carried on a welded trestle from circular hollow sections. Note the Chevaux-de-frise (anti-trespass guard) fanned out across the top of the pipes above the wing wall (at Stechford, ex-LNWR).

L. Wood

Figure 188

Another view of the same structure, together with other lineside items.

L. Wood

Figure 189

A circular refuge built into a brick viaduct. Note the guard rails to prevent derailed vehicles straying, once off the track (near Rectory Junction, ex-GNR).

L. Wood

Figure 190
A view of a private subway formed from longitudinal trough girders almost beneath the station footbridge. Cast-iron columns support the roof over the platforms (at Crewe, ex-LNWR).

L. Wood

Figure 191
The corner of the brickwork of an abutment supporting cast-iron parapets. An ex-Southern Railway bridge numberplate can be seen (near Exeter Central, ex-LSWR).

L. Wood

Figure 192

If the modeller does not wish to build a footbridge or any other form of bridge, here is a simple subway (at Leeds) formed from rectangular hollow sections for posts and timber rails. As concrete slabs were used, there are no physical signs of this subway (unlike that at Crewe) in the platform walls.

L. Wood

Figure 194

A bracket signal attached to the buttress of a bridge. Note the layout of coursed masonry (at Teignmouth Quay, ex-GWR).

L. Wood

Figure 193

An ex-Metropolitan Railway bridge numberplate (near Great Missenden).

L. Wood

Figure 195

To carry a footpath around the edge of an adjacent school, this cantilevered structure was constructed by the GCR, near Gorton.

L. Wood

Figure 196 A view of the well-known struts at Roade, where the line to Northampton drops away from the main line to Rugby. These provide resistance to the walls closing together in the deep cutting. Similar cast-iron struts are visible in the partially open sections of the Circle line in London.

Authors Collection

Figure 197 Similar struts, formed as segmental masonry arches (near Chorley, ex-L&YR).

British Rail

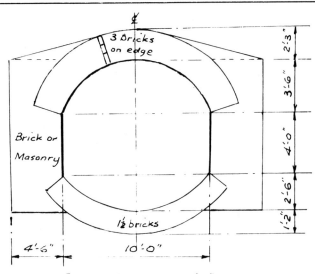

3 Bricks
on edge

Brick or
Masonry

½ bricks

2'-3"

3'-6"

4'-0"

2'-6"

½'-2"

4'-6"   10'-0"

CROSS SECTION :- 10'-0" CULVERT

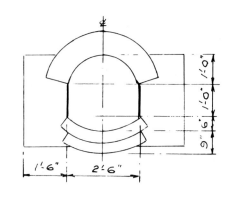

9"
9"
6'-9"
9"
2'-3"

9"   1'-6"

CROSS SECTION : 1'-6" CULVERT

8mm : 1'-0"

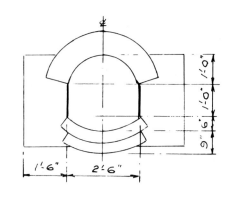

9"
1'-0"
1'-0"

9"
6'-9"

1'-6"   2'-6"

CROSS SECTION : 2'-6" CULVERT

8mm : 1'-0"

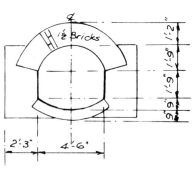

½ Bricks

1'-2"
1'-9"
1'-9"

9"
9"

2'-3"   4'-6"

CROSS SECTION : 4'-6" CULVERT

N.B. FOR 4'-6" CULVERTS OR LARGER, SIDE WALLS
& HEADWALLS COULD BE BRICK OR MASONRY,
SMALLER SIZES WOULD PROBABLY BE
BRICK ONLY

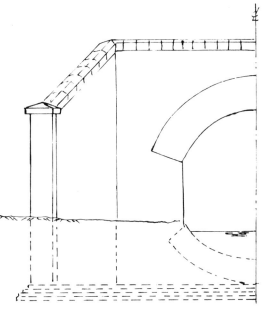

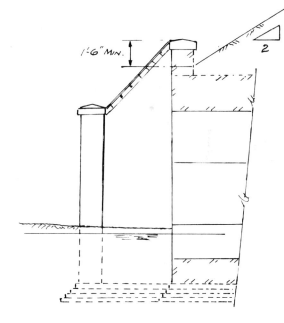

1'-6" MIN.

2

TYPICAL HEADWALL DETAIL

(WINGWALLS COULD BE CURVED)

A series of brick culverts of various spans, for the modeller to
select his own!

Figure 198

Figure 199 Circular brick arch culvert (3 rings) (near Helsby).

Author's Collection

Figure 200 The same culvert, following its reconstruction in 1953 in spun R. C. pipes.

Authors' Collection

Figure 201 Headwall of a 4 ring segmental brick culvert, during maintenance cleaning (near Great Bridge).

British Rail

Figure 202 Gothic-shaped arch forming part of a widened bridge at Banbury.

L. Wood

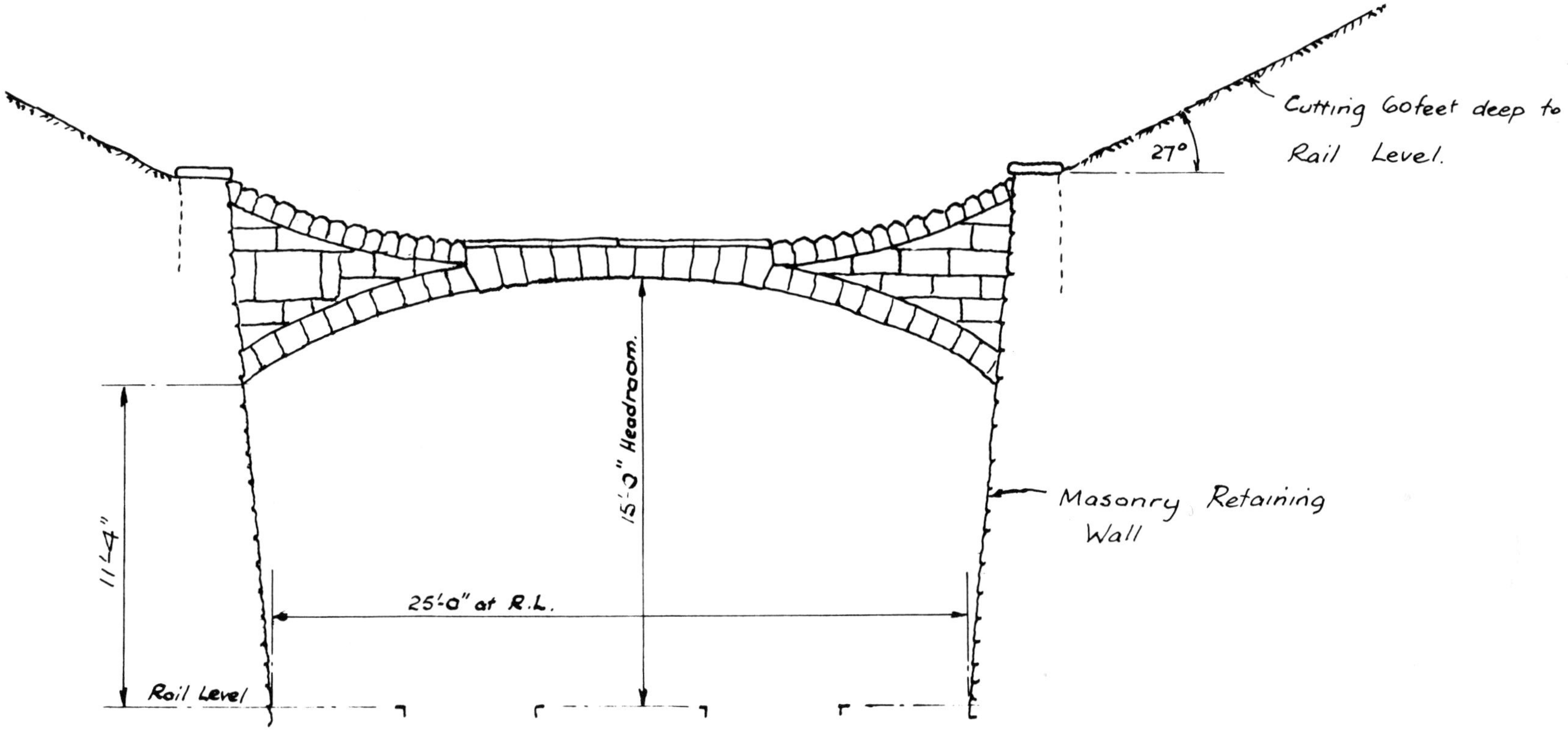

Cutting 60 feet deep to Rail Level.

27°

15'-0" Headroom.

Masonry Retaining Wall

11'-4"

25'-0" at R.L.

Rail Level

This illustration is of the flying masonry arches near Chorley —
an interesting idea instead of providing tunnels (**see Figure 197**).

Figure 203

Figure 204 South face of Old Harecastle Tunnel near Kidsgrove — shaped concrete voussoirs and headwalls.

British Rail

Figure 206 The fast line tunnel mouth at the North end of Primrose Hill tunnel.

British Rail

Figure 205 Circular tunnels carrying the Watford/Broad Street D. C. line at South Hampstead.

British Rail

Figure 207 Clifton Hall Tunnel during engineering work. Note the ventilator inlet and duct to change the air inside the tunnel.

British Rail

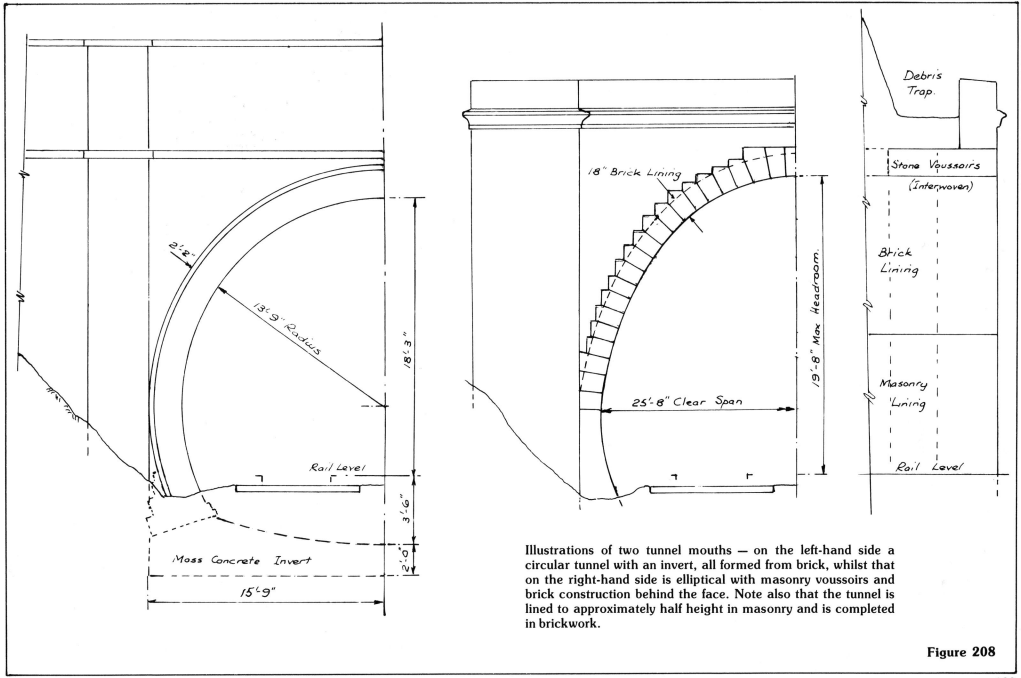

2'-2"

13'-9" Radius

18'-3"

Rail Level

3'-6"

2'-0"

Moss Concrete Invert

15'-9"

18" Brick Lining

25'-8" Clear Span

19'-8" Max Headroom.

Debris Trap.

Stone Voussoirs (Interwoven)

Brick Lining

Masonry Lining

Rail Level

Illustrations of two tunnel mouths — on the left-hand side a circular tunnel with an invert, all formed from brick, whilst that on the right-hand side is elliptical with masonry voussoirs and brick construction behind the face. Note also that the tunnel is lined to approximately half height in masonry and is completed in brickwork.

Figure 208

Glossary of Terms

A

Abutment — Part of a substructure from which the bridge is supported. Built from brick, masonry or concrete.

Angle — Rolled 'L'-shaped section.

Arch — Concave construction of stone, bricks or concrete, built or turned on a contouring over an open space.

B

Beam — Length of timber or rolled section of steel; common word for a concrete unit other than a slab.

Bearing — Point at which a spanning member is supported.

Bedcourse — Concrete or stone unit used for supporting several members (also cill beam).

Bedplate — Steel plate forming lower portion of a bearing sitting on the top of a bedstone.

Bedstone — Large stone or concrete block supporting a girder bearing. Used to spread the load through the abutment.

Bracing — Normally metallic, and helps to tie the main members together (e.g. overhead bracing to truss girder bridges).

C

Camber — Most bridges are made with an inbuilt camber so that when loaded this camber should disappear, due to the deflection. It always appears better than a sag under superimposed load conditions.

Channel — Rolled Z-shaped section.

Chevaux de Frise — Anti-trespass guard; fanned out pointed spikes to prevent trespass along the top of a pipe, bridges or up OLE masts.

Cill beam — See Bedcourse.

Cleat — Small metallic bracket connecting members.

Column — Occasionally used to support a bridge but more usually braced to form a trestle (**see also Pier**)

Composite Construction — Structure built by using both steel sections and concrete units.

Construction Depth — Distance between soffit of bridge at either rail or road level (**see diagram, Figure 2**).

Contraction — Shortening movement of a structure as temperature decreases.

Coping — Stone or concrete capping to wing walls or pilasters.

Corbel — Stepping out of the course of brick or stonework to produce or reduce thickness.

Cover plate — Additional plate to cover joint in construction.

D

Deflection — Amount that member moves downwards when subjected to a superimposed load.

Diaphragm — Stiff member joining two main members together; usually only a short length as opposed to Bracing.

E

Expansion — Lengthening movement of a structure as temperature increases.

Extrados — Outer surface of an arch.

F

Flange — Top or bottom portion of a girder; normally flat but occasionally indus.

Flange Angles — In riveted construction, the portion used to connect the flange plate(s) to the web.

G

Girder — Assembly of metallic flange plates angles and web with suitable stiffening.

Going — Horizontal tread dimension of a staircase.

Grillages — Assembled formation of beams bolted or welded together and placed to form a bearing.

H

Hammer blow — Dynamic loading to bridges caused by the reciprocating motion on a steam locomotive.

I

Intrados — Interior line or the curve of an arch.

Invert — Floor of an arch or tunnel (not always provided).

In situ — Refers to concrete work placed at site (i.e. not pre-cast).

J

Jack Arch — Small arch up to about 5ft. span set between adjacent cross girders (sometimes called jack arch girders).

Joist — Rolled 'I' section.

K

Keystone — Central voussoir stone at the peak of an arch; sometimes placed last and left more prominent.

L

Lattice — Open type framework of flats or rolled sections.

Longitudinal timbers — Long sleepers placed directly under the rail as opposed to normal cross sleepers.

M

Masonry — Normally refers to anything constructed in stone.

O

Outrigger — Support from the bottom flange of a girder to strengthen the top flange. Either formed by a triangle or occasionally curved.

P

Parapet — Formed upstand to prevent people/vehicles falling off the side of a structure.

Pilaster — Small wall, either of brick, masonry or concrete, usually with a coping stone, to retain the fill at the end of the span(s).

Pier — Used where ground conditions are not suitable for normal foundations. Can be timber, concrete or metallic. On timber viaducts, piles usually extend upwards, and are braced to form a trestle.

Pile — Used where ground conditions are not suitable for normal foundations. Can be in timber, concrete or metalallic. On timber viaducts, piles usually extend upwards and are braced to form a trestle or pier.

R

Rail Joint — Fishplated connection in a running rail, normally kept clear of a bridge or welded, if not already continuously welded rail.

Rail bearer — Metallic or timber member spanning a cross girder or from a cross girder to an abutment, located directly under a rail.

Refuge — Safety location formed on long span on viaducts, in the retaining wall or tunnel where limited clearances prevent clearance of a loading gauge.

Riser — Vertical dimension of each stair in a staircase.

Rivet — Made from metal; a bar with one formed head which is heated to red hot, then placed through holes, pre-drilled in a member to be joined and the head at the other end, produced by hammers applied at each end.

S

Soffit — Lowest portion of a bridge span.

Span — Distance between abutments (**see diagram Figure C**).

Spandrel — Irregular triangular shape between an arch ring or a member and the enclosed right-angle.

Springing — Normally triangular-shaped stone from which an arch bridge is supported.

Stiffener — Additional intermediate member to prevent webs of metallic girders from buckling.

String course — Ornamental horizontal line of masonry or brickwork on a bridge or an abutment.

Stringer — Side members of a staircase, either timber or metallic, to support treads.

Substructure — Consists of abutments and foundations of a bridge.

T

Tie Rod — Used as an additional bracing or in a jack arch construction to tie cross girders together to prevent them moving apart.

Transom — Baulk timber placed between longitudinal timbers beneath a rail, held in position by transom bolts.

Trestle — Series of columns or legs braced together to form support for a bridge.

Trough — Early troughs in inverted 'U' form, produced in cast iron, later pressed in wrought iron or steel, or formed in riveted construction by using plate and angles.

V

Voussoir — Wedge-shaped stones forming an arch.

W

Warren girder or truss — Name given to a form of lattice girder with 'N'-shaped bracing.

Web — Vertical member of a girder.

Welding — Joining of two pieces of metal by an electrical arc.

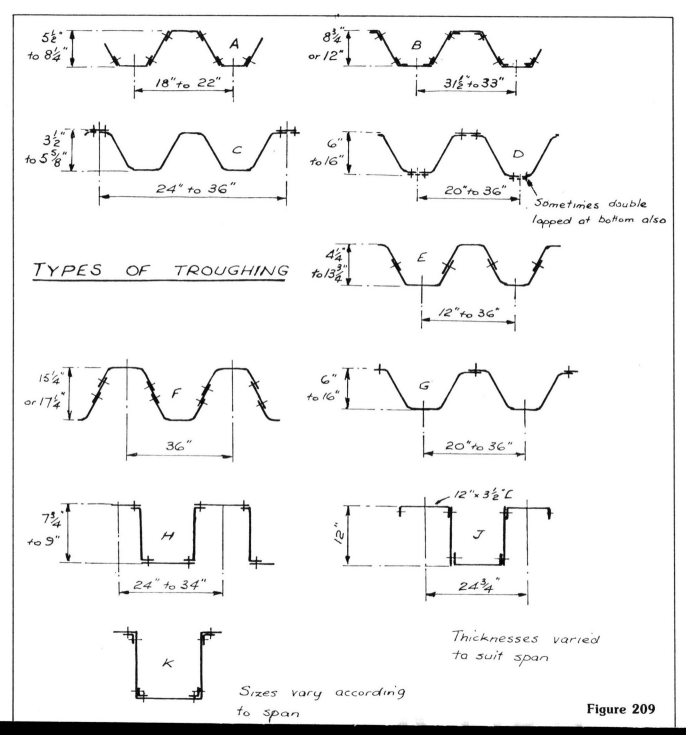

TYPES OF TROUGHING

Figure 209

Types of Troughing

A   Specially shaped Wrought Iron channel with riveted web plates.

B   Specially shaped Wrought Iron angles with riveted web and flange plates.

C   Double section pressed trough with lap plates (riveted or bolted).

D   Lapped pressed troughing (riveted or bolted).

E   Wrought Iron pressed troughing (riveted).

F   Wrought Iron pressed troughing (deeper section, double riveted).

G   Single lap Wrought Iron or Steel troughing (riveted or bolted).

H   Built up box troughing using 'Z' section and flange plates (riveted).

J   Built up box troughing using L section and web plates (riveted).

K   Box troughing, W. I. or steel (riveted) used individually with longitudinal timbers for short span bridges, or joined to form complete transverse deck spanning between main girders.

Model Bridges

In all the popular modelling scales, there is available suitable plastic moundings, like tunnel mouths, which are suitable for producing masonry style bridges. By placing two together, back-filling the parapet and in-filling between the portal, a quite acceptable bridge may easily be produced.

It is also possible to purchase rubber moulds from which modellers may cast their own structures, often done to produce multi-span bridges.

Brick and stone paper, some embossed, are available for overlaying wood or card frames. One manufacturer also supplies brick printed to an arch profile so that either segmental or semi-circular arches may be produced, whilst with a little care an elliptical arch could also be built. Similarly, by using the various modelling clays available, it is possible to overlay wood or card frames to produce a masonry style arch.

Furthermore, embossed brick, coarsed and random stone styrene sheets are also available, should the modeller wish to use these materials. With suitable stiffening, a very strong model can result.

Several proprietary firms produce complete bridge kits, some already painted, although often with careful weathering, a much better model will result. Other manufacturers produce a variety of girders suitable for both underbridges or overbridges. Parapet handrailing may be produced from the small brass angle sections available from many model shops, whilst plastic fencing post could also be used, particularly on a concrete bridge, the holes not required for the hand-railing being filled in.

Girders may also be constructed from styrene sheet. Embossed rivets are produced by one manufacturer, and with care, a well-detailed girder to suit the rivet counter may be constructed!

Several proprietary footbridges are also available, as well as some excellent etched brass structures which, although requiring a little care, produce a superb model.

For the modern image modeller, there is no reason why one of the modern tubular style structures should not be produced, again using the various circular, square and rectangular brass sections, and careful soldering.

Figure 210 A 4mm scale C. I. parapet beam bridge, with vertical timber infill, on the Milton Keynes Model Railway Society's Verney Junction layout (during reconstruction).

A. Daly

Figure 211 A 4mm scale LNWR style lattice footbridge on the MKMRS Verney Junction layout. The girders were built 'flat' on a scale plan and the flanges added later. It is of 'Plastikard' construction.

A. Daly

Figure 212 A 7mm scale metallic overbridge on the author's 'Woodford' layout. Constructed with 'plastikard' girders; brick paper abutments, wingwalls, etc., and shaped balsa wood copings. *A. Daly*

Figure 213 A 7mm scale arch underbridge on the same layout, constructed using modelling clay. Note the culvert with its separate opening on the right. *A. Daly*

Figure 214 The underside of the bridge illustrated in Figure 212, showing the jack arches and internal girders. A lack of rivets on the girders is not really noticeable.

Figure 215 A 7mm scale, 5-ring brick arch overbridge on the same layout. The panels were produced in balsa wood and covered in brick paper. *A. Daly*